T0113349

Awakened
Dreams

Raji's Journeys with the Mirror Dede

Awakened Dreams

Raji's Journeys with the Mirror Dede

Ahmet Hilmi

Translated from the Turkish by
Refik Algan & Camille Helminski

THRESHOLD BOOKS

SHAMBHALA PUBLICATIONS, INC.
Horticultural Hall
300 Massachusetts Avenue
Boston, Massachusetts 02115
www.shambhala.com

Printed in the United States of America

Distributed in the United States by Random House, Inc.,
and in Canada by Random House of Canada Ltd

LIBRARY OF CONGRESS CATALOGING-IN-PUBLICATION DATA

Ahmet Hilmi Sehbenderzade, 1865–1913
    [Amâk-i hayâl. English]
    Awakened dreams : Raji's journey with the Mirror Dede / Ahmet Hilmi :
    translated from the Turkish by Refik Algan & Camille Helminski. p. 160
    ISBN 0-939660-45-8: $13.00
    1. Sufism—Fiction.   I. Title.
PL248.A31723A8313   1993   93-18487
894'.3533—dc20   CIP
BVG 01

Contents

The First Book

The Second Book

*Stories from the Notebook of the Mirror Dede**

*These headings did not appear in the original text but have been incorporated here for formatting clarity.

This translation is dedicated:

To my beloved Nancy Wright.
R.A.

To my beloved husband, my companion on the way, Kabir.
C.A.H.

IN THE NAME OF GOD, THE BENEFICENT AND MERCIFUL,

God! There is no deity but He,
the Ever-Living, the Self-Subsisting Source of All Being.
No slumber can seize Him nor sleep.
All things in heaven and earth are His.
Who could intercede in His presence without His permission?
He knows what appears in front of and behind His creatures.
Nor can they encompass any knowledge of Him
except what He wills.
His throne extends over the heavens and the earth,
and He feels no fatigue in guarding and preserving them,
for He is the Highest and Most Magnificent.

The Throne Verse [Surah Al-Baqarah II:255]

Introduction

*A*wakened Dreams was written by Ahmet Hilmi at the turn of the century. Born in 1865 in what is now Bulgaria but was then under Ottoman rule, Hilmi grew up under the influence of varied cultures. As his father was well-positioned as a consul of the empire, Hilmi was able to receive an excellent education and at an early age began to inquire into the nature of existence. He became fluent in several languages and aware of intellectual and philosophical developments in many parts of the world.

While still a young man Hilmi moved with his family to Izmir, Turkey, where he met the Mirror Dede (*Dede* is an affectionate term for grandfather or respected elder), a "cosmic doctor" who was living in relative anonymity in a local cemetery. Through companionship with the Mirror Dede and the influence of his mystical music, a new world of meaning opened for Hilmi as he passed through transformational experiences which are reflected here in the text of *Awakened Dreams*. *Awakened Dreams* is a depiction of the process of Sufism, the process of coming into unity of Being with the deep awareness that all of nature, and human beings and their activities are derived from and reflect the one Source, or God.

A contemporary teacher in the Sufi tradition, Metin Bobaroglu, in speaking about the importance of *Awakened Dreams*, said:

> "Works such as *Awakened Dreams*, created within the field
> of Sufism, were produced as a result of inner experiences and
> portray Being comprehended by Essence rather than by in-

tellect alone. Reason and intuition come together in understanding and the living of Truth within Divine Love.

In Sufism, great importance is given to the complete human being, the one who is considered to have the qualities and attributes of God completely activated. It is through the guidance of such a human being that the inner process unfolds. Any particular beliefs in dogmas dissolve as the complete one assists the seeker to fall fully into his or her relationship with God and to recognize the importance of that essential experience.

The spiritual journey is essentially the same for every seeker from the point of view of the stages of the ego. Within the Sufi tradition it is recognized that each soul passes through seven stages of development as it is refined in its ability to merge with the Divine. However, from the point of view of manifestation, this process is unique for each traveler; one should not expect the same manifestations as those of someone else. In Sufism—or simply, the unfolding of Truth—the process of spiritual evolution is referred to as *Seyr-i-suluk*,[1] which means "all that is seen and experienced by a seeker from the beginning of her or his spiritual journey until its end."

On the way through the stages of evolution, the spiritual journey is evaluated according to the spiritual dreams which the traveler sees. Within this tradition it is understood that no matter what or with whom particular dreams may be related, they reflect the state of the seer or dreamer. It is emphasized that these dreams should only be evaluated by a mature guide in order that they may be used as guidance for the journeyor."

Though it has all the elements of a fantastic fairy tale, *Awakened Dreams* is not a fantasy but a real transcription of the spiritual journey. For many years now it has been used by teachers in many branches of Sufism within Turkey as a means of reflecting on the state of an individual's progress on "the path of return," the return of the human being to his or her Source, and unity with God.

---

1. *Seyr-i-suluk*: *Seyr* (Arabic): to wander about, to see, to watch. *Suluk* (Arabic): to set out on a way; to forge ahead.

Ahmet Hilmi himself went on to become a teacher in the Arusi branch of Sufism. He continued throughout his life to work towards the manifestation of a society governed by Spirit. For him, this vision reflected the Islamic Sufi framework within which he matured. He taught philosophy at Istanbul University and published over forty books, as well as several weekly papers and magazines. When writing about ideas of Sufism, he used the pen name, Shaikh Mehridden Arusi. When writing political articles, he used the name Uzdemir, or The Iron One. His many humorist writings were penned under the name The Exuberant Kalendar (wandering ascetic). Hilmi was exiled several times for his activism against the Sultanate, and was eventually poisoned in 1914 during the final years of intrigue of the Ottoman Empire. He died at the age of forty-nine.

The visionary experiences narrated in *Awakened Dreams* weave a timeless tapestry; in order to help the reader follow the story, it would seem helpful to share a brief time line.

The story begins with a dissolute young Raji meeting the Mirror Dede in a cemetery (home to those who no longer exist. The ultimate aim of the process of Sufism is to die before death, to assist the melting of the individual ego within the unity of Being, of God). Through companionship with the Mirror Dede, Raji finds a means to begin this process of unfolding and melting which will satisfy the longing of his soul. Day after day, the Mirror Dede helps facilitate Raji's transformational experience. Then after the ninth day (the number of completion), Raji is left on his own. Yet this is only the mid-point of the narrative. Here, the second book begins after a lapse of several years during which it appears that Raji attempted to convey to others some of the knowledge and experience he had incorporated. However, we now find him in a state of extreme bewilderment. At this point, the Mirror Dede reappears and Raji continues the process of proving within himself that existence and nonexistence are the same. Through companionship with the Mirror Dede and his own consistent, sincere effort, Raji's being ripens into Unity; the lover and Beloved become One. Raji then shares with us a few stories from the perspective of the Mirror Dede. Through these last stories we are ultimately led full circle back into the "happiness" of living and dying as an "ordinary," balanced human being of good morality. The book ends with the recital of prayers by orphans for the blessing of their benefactor. The traditional prayer offered here, the Fatiha, is the prayer for beginnings as well . . . "We begin in the Name of God, the Compassionate and Merciful," and before God we are all orphans returning to our Source, and He alone is our Benefactor and the Source to which we are returning. Existence continues to cycle.

In the words of the Mirror Dede:

"O Oneness! You are the endless, rolling sea!
Again it is You who is seen among the many waves. Though You have given Yourself a thousand names, a hundred thousand forms, whatever is said—the sky, the stars, the spirit of the body—is You, only You!

Even if the eye of man looks with intense attention at the universe—the sky, the blue vault, the sun, the world above, or this earth and this lowly soil—even if he looks at the face of Adam with the telescope of knowledge, it is You, only You!

In hyacinth and basil, or in thistle; in the heart-rending roar of the lion, or the sweet voice of the nightingale; in the bud that lends joy, or the fragrance of the rose that uplifts the spirit; in the most lifeless particle; in the least of the animals; it is You, only You!

In all my senses; in heart, intellect, and conscience; when I am drunk and bewildered with the desire of love; and in the pain of the moments when I am separated from my beloved; in my uncertain soul that burns with longing—it is You, only You!

In my embrace, when the moon-faced beauty trembles; when in a moment infinity unfolds; when enraptured, I behold the snowy sky; in fear of grandeur when my soul is bewildered—it is never anything but You, only You!"

Love is returning us to Itself.

Camille Helminski
Putney, Vermont

Awakened
Dreams

CHAPTER ONE

Waters-Edge

*F*or quite some time I had been living in one of Turkey's most famous cities. If you walked through its central district, between the government office where I worked and my house, your attention might be snagged by any number of things: numerous old houses, crumbling ruins, streets so filled with the bustling of humanity they appeared impossible to cross, obscure passageways . . . but the place that always caught my curiosity was an old cemetery near my home.

Massive but graceful walls surrounded it. About every ten meters, window openings spanned by unusual bronze bars punctuated the thick walls. The original entrance gate, fallen into ruin long ago, had been replaced by a simple wooden one, but original art work still adorned the tombs where memories and corpses lay buried. I could see beautiful calligraphy on the gravestones as I peered through the barred windows. It was easy to tell by the quality of its rendering that it had been carved by old masters of the art. Not only was it beautiful, but at a glance you could perceive that it was true poetry. Carved conical hats, wrapped turbans, and crowns capped the tops of the stones and made me wonder about the histories they marked.

1

Long abandoned, this cemetery held a strange charm. Poison hemlocks as tall as a man, said to emit the odor of the dead, overspread the grounds in early summer. Once it had been at the outskirts, but as the city expanded, it had been swallowed up by civilization.

Everyday I passed and would think of visiting, but young men like me, who spend half their precious time earning a living and the other half entertaining themselves, have little time left for cemeteries. My free time was already so filled with meaningless activities that each day I could spare but a moment to admire the ordered strength of the walls; I could never take the time to actually enter.

In order for you to understand my situation, I should tell you a bit about my life. As I had been raised with the infinite care of a virtuous, religious mother, I had a deeply rooted sense of both religion and virtue. I had received the best education available and, since I had a gift for learning, soon knew a great deal more than most people my age. After finishing my formal schooling, rather than putting aside my studies like most young people, I attempted to increase my knowledge. I sought out information about everything, including religious sciences which my friends avoided. I was drawn to absorb everything, especially esoteric ideas. Yet one day, after examining my conscience under this heap of information, I realized how confused I was. I was stuffed with both belief and unbelief, faith and denial, acceptance and suspicion. I was confirming with my intellect that which I denied with my heart and confirming with my heart that which I denied with my intellect. The dragon of doubt had captured me. It didn't matter how well I constructed an idea; doubt could crush it with a single blow. Even a complete denial couldn't bring me peace, for doubt was the enemy of any idea; it didn't matter whether it was an affirmation or a denial; this beast wouldn't embrace it.

I found myself caught in a terrible agony. Things which were normal for everyone else were not so for me. Since outer life is often a reflection of one's inner state, you might guess that I was most unfortunate in love and in my attempts to earn a living. I had become someone who kept himself aloof.

In this unbearable situation I discovered that I could find some relief in drunken rapture, but with continuous drinking, my body was becoming dissolute and wretched. One day, mustering all my inner strength, I managed to extricate myself from this foolishness. I re-embarked on my search for knowledge hoping that I would discover evidence which would help me to kill this dragon of doubt. I sought out esoteric specialists. I found people of amazing virtue, but what can I say? In my opinion, their knowledge and proofs were nothing but primitive mythologies. To save myself from the impasse at which I now found myself, it was crucial that I find someone who could refute all my conglomerated knowledge and clearly demonstrate the truths they claimed. I met no such person.

There were two clubs in this city devoted to Western experiments. One of them, a spiritualist association, was interested in necromancy, including strange entertainments like turning tables. I questioned some of the most dedicated members who spoke of their firm belief in the existence of the spirit, but the proofs they demonstrated held no validity for me. After that I connected with members of the club involved with hypnotism. I found myself wondering what I could really gain from such things. Once a man has obtained worldly property, he begins to want strange powers as well, but strange powers weren't important to me; I was looking for something else.

This second period of investigation brought me no real clarity. Instead, everything new I learned became more food for the doubt-dragon. Now with renewed strength it promptly flung me aside, and this time I fell into hell itself. Waves of opposing ideas roared through my brain, creating constant turmoil. My mental anguish reached such an intensity that once again I sought relief in intoxication and frivolity; I became the outrageous ringleader of my most flirtatious and debauched friends. At least this jangling noise of eating and drinking numbed me, bringing me a superficial happiness.

I drank. . . . I drank continuously.

Now just because I describe my friends as "flirtatious" and "debauched," don't assume they were vile or dishonorable. On the contrary, they were honest, well-educated young people of clear conscience, but they had become addicted to entertainment and sensual pleasure;

3

they had set out on the Way of Indifference. Most of them spent their time pursuing their professions or whatever personal interests they had, but none of them ever expressed any wish to understand the puzzle of existence. Some of them even lived as though spiritual feeling were completely nonexistent, viewing religion and philosophy as mythological residue. What a strange opinion! I used to be envious that they could feel so oblivious. Other friends were Muslims who only remembered they were Muslims when they saw the lamps lit for Ramadan.[1] When the lamps were aglow, their prayer beads in their hands, they made the rounds of the mosques where the Qur'an was read and sermons were delivered; they would listen to everything, but understood nothing. They even used to fast, but only if they waited until late afternoon to arise which meant their fast only lasted a few hours. Some thought it wasn't necessary to do the five daily prayers, even though they would observe the daily fast in their own limited way. None of them seemed willing to do the *tarawih*, the extended night prayer. When Ramadan came to an end, their religious feeling evaporated. Every year I was shocked to witness such seasonal piety, like clothing that quickly changes when the weather shifts.

One pleasant spring day, some of my friends suggested a jaunt in the country. After a long debate we decided to go for three days beyond the outskirts of the city to a small town known for its beauty. A railroad line connected it to the center of the city, so after gathering together the things we would need but wouldn't be able to find there, we boarded the train.

The outskirts of the city were quite open, and the fertile land through which the train passed was especially charming. As we journeyed, the lovely panorama induced a raucous joy in my friends, but I found myself caught by a deep sorrow. What use is unusual beauty when it has neither consistency nor permanency? Does eternity belong to man who is but one spectator and witness of this beauty among

---

1. Ramadan: the Islamic holy month dedicated to fasting and the intensification of prayer, as well as the sharing of brotherhood. One fasts from sunrise to sunset, engages in prayer at the usual five prayer times, and if one is dedicated, remains in prayer long into the night.

thousands of creatures? Is it possible to look at this temporary home we call "the earth" without being caught by a deep sorrow? Where did we come from? Where are we going? A pure belief might have beautiful answers for these questions, but reason and science were silent. I looked out over the fields again. This time the unique beauty of nature had disappeared. The light had fled, and darkness had invaded everything. The horrible truth had become painfully apparent: the comforting green of the grass is nothing but a play of light; the myriad bird songs are only vibrations of air. This light spreading over the universe is only a vibrating wave! We are all the slaves of a natural law! It was as if Gautama Buddha took shape in front of me and with his pale smile was saying "Nothing! Nothing! Nothing!"

A friend who noticed how thoughtful I had become asked, "What's the matter with you now?"

"Nothing." I answered. This "nothing" that spilled off my lips not only explained my situation at that moment but also expressed what I saw as the solitary attribute of the whole universe. My friends, bothered by my silent sorrow, began to show their disapproval. The sad countenance appropriate for a funeral is not tolerated for long at a party. One friend spoke up, "We forgot the medicine," and filled my glass. No one could be more joyful than I was after I had emptied this cup five times.

In the late afternoon with great exuberance we arrived at our destination. This small village is the most beautiful I have ever seen. In fact I was so attracted to it that if it had been possible I would have moved there. The houses of the town are located with considerable space between them, each surrounded by a garden of almost an acre. Many streams flow through the gardens, and larger streams flow along parallel with some of the streets. The gardens are all full of fruit trees. Roses grow profusely there, and when they are in bloom, nightingales abound. In short, the town is a paradise on earth.

When we arrived at the station, we were welcomed by a friend whom we had visited a few times before. We spent the night at his house, and the following morning he took us to a place called "Water's-edge." The charming song of the water caressed our ears as it bubbled up in clear springs, overflowed into a natural pond, and spilled out again into many small streams.

We located the most beautiful place to settle ourselves, but two strange people had already arrived there before us. They appeared to be vagabonds, beggars, drunkards, or perhaps dervishes. Despite their presence we sat down. These shabby ones paid no attention to us; they were speaking with each other. As if we were a figment of the imagination, we drew not even a glance from them. The "As-salamu aleykum" greeting of peace of one of our friends evaporated into the air unanswered.

Everyone in our party began to busy themselves. Some began cooking, others prepared the appetizers, while I approached the large wicker-wrapped drinking bottle, deciding to numb my mind again. By chance this brought me near the shabby ones, and I began to listen to their conversation.

The older one, who appeared to be about fifty, was speaking, and the younger one was listening and asking questions from time to time. Their conversation at first led me to think they were insane, or perhaps "Majdhubs," holy fools of God. It was odd that they were speaking about the same subjects which for some time had been disturbing me. The older one was saying to the younger: "Whatever exists in this universe is my attribute. If I had not existed, nothing would exist. I am everything or nothing. I am nothing or everything. As a matter of fact, 'nothing' and 'everything' are both the one-eyed, single thing; it is just the ignorant masses who have named one thing with two names!" Their conversation continued in a similar manner.

I was amazed. Somewhat reluctantly, I interrupted them: "How strange! Can being and nothingness be the same? For instance, now I exist, but tomorrow I will not exist. Is there not a difference between these two states?" The mad one turned his head around to look at me and burst out laughing: "Oh! So, you exist, eh! One wonders if you *do* exist."

I had asked myself this question many times. If I do exist, why will I be nonexistent? If I won't be nonexistent, will my spirit remain eternally? Well, this is where the dragon of doubt reared its fiery head. Will my spirit exist eternally? What is spirit? Is it sensitive by itself? Can its identity be known? If it exists, what will its situation be when it leaves the mold of the body?

Here were a lot of questions for which I had no answer. The mad one continued: "Only I exist, because I am nothing, nonexistent. My body is absolute. Nonexistence exists in that which is under restriction. The absolute is the only being. It is existent."

After this the mad man stopped speaking. No matter what I said, I could get no reply. Finally, he grew tired of my questions and said to his friend, "Let's go. This animal has kept us from our pleasure." They stood up and left. What a strange situation! A shabby madman had called a perfectly educated human being "an animal"!

As planned we remained in the small town for three days. In spite of my friends' complaints and persistent efforts to divert me, I spent the entire three days in apathetic silence. When we boarded the return train, one of my friends spoke to me about something, but paying no attention to what he was saying, I continued having a heart-to-heart talk with my own thoughts. Involuntarily, words came out of my mouth, and I heard myself say to my friend, "I wonder if I exist?" He burst into laughter, "Pass the raki fast; Raji's about to go crazy!"

Two days after we returned, I was passing by the cemetery on the way to the café when I noticed that the gate stood open, which was unusual. Recognizing an opportunity, with a great longing welling up in my heart, I went inside. I walked in the shade of ancient, tall trees. As I tred upon the huge plants that commonly grow in cemeteries, the smell of the dead wafted through the air.

Some of the trees planted in a circle in the middle of the cemetery drew my attention, and I walked over to sit among them for a while. As I approached, I saw that they surrounded a group of graves belonging to a single large family. When I entered the circle, I came upon a hut built of mats and pieces of wood leaning against one of the trees. I was just about to open its door, thinking the hut was abandoned, when a man in old shabby clothing came out.

He looked about fifty and wore a green cap embellished with forty or fifty small mirrors. On his tattered robe, the cloth of which resembled a rainbow with lots of patches, little mirrors or tinplates shimmered as he moved through the dappled light. His appearance was so strange I found it difficult not to laugh, but his gaze upon me was so charmingly soft and humble and his countenance held such a sad calmness that, instead of laughing, I was moved to step respectfully towards him. With a seriousness quite in contrast to his clothing, he spoke slowly, with a harmonious voice, "Welcome, O Light[2] of my eyes! Come in, please!" Whereupon he took a piece of mat out from inside his hat and spread it out on the ground. I sat down.

In front of us were about fifteen gravestones inscribed with beautiful calligraphy; on our right and on our left, the trees grew closely together. My strange host went inside the hut and brought out an earthen pot used as a brazier. Then he returned inside, this time coming out with an old coffee box, a pot with a long handle for making Turkish coffee, two coffee cups, a pitcher, a tobacco box, and a few other tin boxes. He drew the coffee pot to the fire which he had burning with dry grass and some garbage. "Welcome, my Light, how are you? You are well?" he inquired.

"Praise be to God!" I answered.

The great contrast between this man's sincere manner and the absurdity of his clothing continued to surprise me. He spoke to me again, "What is your name?"

"Ahmet Raji," I replied.

He smiled, "'Ahmet Raji?' You have taken the name of mankind, my Light. Mankind is so incapable, weak, and needy that he continues his life by entreaty. 'Raji' means 'human.'"

Hearing these words, I was all the more astonished. I asked, "What is your name?"

"I have many names. People call me by different names in different places. Because of the mirrors I wear, here I am called 'The Mirror Dede.'[3] But call me 'Father Adam' if you would like."

I thought for a while, and then without restraining myself, I spoke,

2. *Nur*: one of the qualities of God—the One who provides light to the whole universe, including the hearts and minds of men and womenkind.

3. Dede: Grandfather; a term of respect and endearment used for an elder of great wisdom.

"Oh, sir, it's obvious that you are one of those who have reached maturity. I can't understand why you hide yourself under this strange clothing."

"It's very simple," he replied after pouring some coffee into my cup. "Everyone is fond of finery. People spend lots of money to have special clothes made. This is the kind of clothing I enjoy."

This answer was both sensible and nonsensical. I thought about it and didn't find it sensible enough. I told him so, and he replied: "You don't find my thesis sensible; but why not? If people find it sensible when a fifty-year-old man buys a halter for himself and calls it a 'necktie,' why should the mirror pieces I attach to my ears be nonsensical? Let us assume that both indicate the absurdity and insanity of mankind; even then, my insanity is more luminous and more logical."

Suddenly an idea dawned in my mind. I wanted to speak about serious matters with this Mirror Dede who might possibly be a philosopher disguised as a lunatic, so I said, "O Sultan, you are a treasure buried in a place of ruins, and I am an idle one who is thirsty for philosophy. Will you please let me learn from you? Let me kiss your hand.⁴"

"Kiss my hand?" he asked with astonishment, "Why? Let's talk if you want to. But what comes from words? Who knows how many libraries of books you have read; what did you understand? What is all this knowledge of mankind but developments to satisfy individual needs and pleasures. What do men really know of the Truth? It's possible to acknowledge that which is true with an equation of the intellect, but is it possible to really know, to understand and realize? Well, what shall we speak about? Can the essence of philosophy be known through a series of letters?"

The reality of these words of a lunatic, in such odd clothes, belittling the knowledge of a great civilization, which I had honored for so long, made me feel inadequate and humble. My mind went blank. Smiling at my dilemma, he said, "Let's leave tiring assumptions aside and get enraptured, shall we?"

Together the Mirror Dede and I each drank another cup of coffee.

4. to kiss the hand: a traditional way of honoring an elder or of showing respect and commitment to a teacher.

CHAPTER TWO

The First Day:
The Hill of Nothingness

Nirvana, Nirvana?!..
Gautama Buddha

*A*fter we drank our coffee, the Mirror Dede brought a ney[1] out from his hut and began to play softly. The silence combined with the sad voice of the ney washed me with an unfamiliar pleasure. Of course the coffee also had an effect, contributing to a strange delight which gradually became more and more powerful. Sighs escaped me, sometimes joyful, sometimes sad. I felt something inside myself shift, as if a heavy load that I had been doomed to carry was being taken away. A new buoyancy filled me. When the Mirror Dede ended his improvisation, he began to sing in a low voice:

> O Soul! Throw a glance at this souvenir
>> of nothingness and learn a lesson.
> End heedlessness and sleep;
>> appearances aren't empty.
> Where is the Great Alexander or Solomon the King?

1. ney: a reed flute.

Live a hundred thousand lives
    in a moment, joyfully.
O my eye! Neither the rose
    nor the nightingale inherits
    the vineyard of the universe infinitely.
With whom did this whirling universe
    become a lover willingly?

When the Mirror Dede stopped singing and once more began to play the ney, tears were streaming from my eyes. I don't know whether these were tears of longing and grief, or tears of love and pleasure; I only knew that I was immensely sad. It's not possible to explain my state of mind and consciousness in that moment. The Mirror Dede was singing again:

Don't obey greed or rage;
    don't be defeated by the flesh.
Comfort doesn't last;
    don't let your name be famous.
Attain the conversation of a saint;
    don't vanish.
Of worldly renown
    don't be proud.

His voice was now hardly audible, as if it were coming from very far away, and the ney had acquired quite a bewildering sound.

The Perfected Ones weren't deceived
    by the pleasures of the world.
They realized that all of this
    is but a shadow play.
The sweet wrapping of the universe
    soon melts away
Holding the skirt of love,
    some have reached the lover.

My awareness weakened as the Mirror Dede's voice grew more and more distant. Gradually I shed sensation altogether, or rather, my external existence; I neither saw nor heard anything. For a while I remained in a state close to sleep, but then mental activity began again, and without yet feeling anything externally, I began to see myself in a strange world, plunged into the depths of imagination. Though my eyes were closed, I could see. . . .

I was on an open plain unlike our own country. The field was covered with tall rush-like grass through which various animals were wandering. Though some were wild beasts, I wasn't afraid but, without hesitation, proceeded on my way. A friend accompanied me and spoke with me from time to time, but I was unable to see him. When it was necessary to ask about something, I asked and was answered. We walked on for hours.

Becoming tired, I asked my friend, who apparently was also my servant, where we were going. "We are in India on our way to the Hill of Nothingness," he replied. Acquiescing to his guidance, I continued. After some time had passed, an extremely high mountain appeared in front of us. Some time later, when we had reached the base of it, a hut beside a small stream came into sight.

My friend told me to go towards the hut, so I did. As I approached it, a young man came out and asked me what I wanted.

I didn't know what I wanted, but my companion answered for me, "I brought him to visit the Hill of Nothingness. Please guide him."

The young man's face lit up with happiness as he looked at me; he took my hand and said simply, "Come." After leading me to sit in the shade of a tall tree, he spoke, "Only one in a thousand or a hundred thousand can climb the Hill of Nothingness, because in order to ascend that hill, one must be master of oneself. If there is a single desire in your heart, you lose your way and cannot go further. Only the living dead can ascend this hill. Do you feel such a purity within yourself?" I replied that, to the contrary, I was a weak and impatient man, who knew desire well. "What a pity!" he said. "Most people are like this, but let's try it once anyway. Perhaps we shall succeed."

Taking my hand, he led me to the hut."Today you are a guest here. Tomorrow before dawn we'll climb the hill. Let's talk a bit so we don't waste time." He asked my name.

"Raji," I replied. Though I was feeling rather ashamed before this person for whom I had already come to feel a deep respect, I was drawn to ask, "What is your name?"

"Buddha Gautama Shakyamuni," he replied.

Buddha! Respectfully I stood up to kiss his hand. He stopped me and said, "If it is for me that you do this, I am nothing; respect and insult are equal to me. If it is for you, your love from the heart is enough."

Before dawn the next day, we set out. Buddha held my hand. The foothills radiated a charm that seemed unearthly, or perhaps it was just that the charm of this earth is not so often perceived because we usually look about us with unseeing eyes. As we climbed, on either side of the path various green flowers blossomed in abundance. An enrapturing fragrance filled the air, and the singing of the nightingales from among the rose trees awakened strong feelings in my heart. A very fine, golden bright sand as soft as cotton covered our path. The splashing and rippling of small streams flowing along both sides of the path delighted our ears like a lover's whisper. The higher we went, the more charming the surroundings became.

At last we arrived at what appeared to be a small palace. The altitude and fine air had awakened quite an appetite in me. As soon as we entered, the most savory smells wafted towards us, making me feel quite marvelous. In the center of the large room in which we now found ourselves was a table filled with countless foods, exquisitely prepared and set out upon golden plates. I felt a compelling desire to approach the table and eat, but Buddha continued to hold my hand and whispered in my ear: "We are ascending the Hill of Nothingness. If you eat of any of these foods you will have to take leave of me and descend."

In spite of the intense hunger which had taken hold of me, I managed to restrain myself. We sat in front of those delicious foods for a full hour. Buddha kept silent. I felt helpless under the influence of strange feelings. Why was I offered that which was natural to man without being allowed to nourish myself? One had to eat and drink to live. In my mind I began resisting the idea of this person attempting to deny a man's hunger as though he were an angel. Then, suddenly, Buddha spoke, "Let's go. We have relaxed enough."

Just as we were leaving the palace, a young man appeared in front of me. He seemed to be a heavenly servant and carried a golden tray upon which rested three crystal goblets. One was filled with water, another with wine, and the third with sweet nectar. "Master," he addressed me, "the place to which you are ascending is still very far away. You haven't eaten anything. At least drink something, please!"

At once, accepting his gentle entreaty, I picked up the cup of wine. The young man's face filled with a luminous joy as he watched me, but the moment I was to touch the cup to my lips, Buddha hit my hand and the goblet crashed to the floor. Without saying a word, Buddha took my hand again and led me out. We continued on our way.

It was not long before we heard a mysterious voice so beautiful that the voice of the Prophet David would seem false in comparison. It was singing:

> Walk, O idle traveler, walk.
>> Don't linger.
> Don't let the pleasures of the world detain you
>> from union with the Beloved One.
> These novel curiosities, these pleasant tastes
>> are but a dream, imaginary.
> Walk, O helpless visitor, walk.
> Don't linger, walk.
>
> Walk, so that you may delight in Union.
> Walk, die at your origin;
>> this is the way of perfection.
> Walk, leave this display
>> so that the cup of Union may quench your thirst.
> Walk, that you may meet the unfolding
>> within the Field of Nothingness.

Bathed with the sweetness of these words, with tears of sorrow and of enjoyment flowing from my eyes, we journeyed onward. We

14

passed the night upon the grass where I fell into a deep, dreamless sleep. We set out again early the next morning. At midday, another palace appeared in front of us, of the kind one could see only in one's dreams; it would be impossible to even imagine a palace more perfect, more beautiful. When we were within five or ten steps of the entrance, the doors opened automatically.

Buddha spoke: "This palace is where most people's feet slide. It is the place of examination. The ones who hold to the well-braided rope of bravery and constancy are able to continue; further ahead is the Hill of Nothingness. Those distracted by the opulence here fall into the Valley of Hell, overcome with grief and sadness. This is the false paradise of desires and ambitions; further ahead is the Field of Nothingness which has no beginning. Here is a palace of vanity, a guest house which utterly destroys every one of its visitors. Here torments abound. Further on, you come to the absolute universe and the emptiness of true pleasure and freedom, to Unity. To remain here is to be caught in a house of sorrow, to be a slave of desire. The one who goes beyond is freed from self-importance and anxieties. He gains the throne of infinite emptiness that fills the universe. Be brave! Don't be deceived! Endure and be determined! I will be waiting for you here."

Pointing to the door of the palace, he told me, "Go in." Cool, fragrant air soothed me as I walked through the garden which shimmered with jewelled paths, emerald grass, and brilliant flowers. When I reached the door of the palace, twenty or thirty beautiful concubines welcomed me, and with great respect and reverence, I was guided by two of them into an adjoining room. The elaborate ornamentation of the palace astounded and confused me, as did the exquisite beauty of the young women and especially the charm and grace of the ones who took me by the arms.

The young women on one side of this room spoke sorrowfully together; while on the other, they chatted among themselves like singing birds, filling the air with magical encouragement. One held up a cup to me, her lips burning like fire. Bewildered, I drank.

The liquid was ice-cold and more delightful and delicious than any of the refreshments I had ever known. It was as if I had found new life. At once, bundles were brought, and silken towels were unwrapped. With their tiny hands my new servants began to take off my clothes. I was brought into the bath where I was welcomed by numerous naked concubines. Their bodies were so perfect and so erotic that if angels were brought among these bare beauties, the spirit of desire would be awakened even in them. I was laid down for a massage on cushions spread upon the central slab of the bath, which had been formed of various kinds of colored stones. My body trembled from the delicate touches of the concubines; I was really quite tired and soon became so relaxed that I fell into a sweet sleep. Upon awakening I was brought to a hot corner of the bath and washed thoroughly. After having been refreshed with cool water, no fatigue remained in me; my body was completely renewed.

The spring of life and power had served its purpose, and I was taken out of the bath and led into another perfect room. A silver tray graced an ebony table set with jewelled dishes. Delicious foods beyond comparison with any of this world were brought to me. One of the angel-faced concubines brought forward a crystal decanter and presented me with a cup of wine. Several played musical instruments and sang sweet songs. This entertaining assembly lasted for about an hour. My pleasure had reached its peak; my carnal spirit had gone mad and, through the fierceness and wildness of sexual desire, had turned into a dragon. At that moment a beautiful young woman entered. Joining her hands over her breast, she paused in front of me: "Master, the genie who is absent is the genie of love and union. For days she has been waiting for you with eyes full of tears. Come, please."

She took me by the arm and brought me to the second floor of the palace where she ushered me into a room and then closed the door behind me. To my tearful desire, the genie of beauty revealed her face; I couldn't help showing my astonishment. To compare this genie of love with the most beautiful woman in the world was like comparing a candle to the sun.

My eyes were so dazzled that I was unable to see, and my knees could no longer support me. The sexual light radiating from her eyes was so charming, the smile upon her lips so inviting, that I lost the

16

strength to stand. Due to the intensity of my excitement, I could only crawl to the bed, lifting my wet eyes towards her unique beauty, begging for pity. She shone like the moon, encircled with a bright halo. This genie of union lay upon a bed draped with purple satin; only a thin silk blouse obscured her curving body from view. How could such a veil protect that angel face from being fervently admired? The light of desire in her eyes grew more and more brilliant and enticing. Implying hurt as well, her lips began to tremble while her rosy cheeks flamed even brighter with the fire of passion. Her black hair curled about her silvery throat which quivered with deep longing. Such a paragon of beauty could only be made of contrary qualities, but she opened her arms: "Come, come!" she begged me, and moaning my gratitude, I flung myself into her waiting warmth. I embraced that body of light with mine and madly kissed her bright cheeks and trembling lips.

This union lasted but a moment. At once a thunderous sound shook the palace as if an earthquake had split the world. Lightning struck. That great building, those lovely walls, crashed to the ground and melted away like a handful of sugar. Filled with fear, I closed my eyes and held tight to my lover, but when I opened my eyes, I found myself in the lap of an ugly witch. She was so ugly and so dirty, that shrieking in astonishment, hatred, and pain, I tried to tear myself from her embrace. As she burst into owl-like laughter, her chin curled upward, joining her nose, which now was as sharply curved as an eagle's beak. When the two hooks of her face parted, her mouth opened, revealing a filthy hole edged with long yellow teeth. The more I tried to free myself, the more powerfully she encircled me. She railed at me, "You ingrate! You have already forgotten that a moment ago you prostrated yourself at my feet; you've already forgotten the deep pleasure of union you just tasted. After a while I'll appear in that form again."

With great difficulty, I wrenched myself from her arms. The palace was now a rubbish heap; the concubines had become horrible witches who pursued me. Afraid of falling into their clutches, I ran as fast as I could, almost flying. At last, I could run no longer and fell down exhausted, only to discover that the witches had given up and were no longer chasing me. I looked around and began to think. Instead of the emerald grass, I now saw thorns. Instead of nightingales, I saw crows. Instead of golden sand, I saw black, sharp-pointed stones.

I remembered. He would be waiting for me at the door. The door, however, no longer existed, and Buddha had disappeared. Slowly I began to descend the mountain. I arrived at an open area where a majestic assembly appeared in front of me. To the north of the field, Buddha was sitting upon a golden throne, with a golden crown upon his head, a sceptor ornamented with precious stones in his hand, and gilded robes around him. Surrounding him were other people also wearing crowns and brightly ornamented clothing. Two people took me by the arms and brought me closer to his presence. Buddha arose with great dignity. Raising his arm, he pointed his index finger at me: "O man who could not keep your word, O Adam, O you of weak character, pity be upon you! You couldn't arrive where you needed to be. You weren't able to enter the true palace of Unity. You didn't reach absolute union because you couldn't ascend the Hill of Nothingness. O heedless man, leave us! Descend! Go to the ugly faced witch; go to the world in front of whom you prostrated yourself and surrendered your strength and your spirit! You are not the joy of humanity. You are not the stalwart one of this universe. Descend! Let the dragon of desire eat your lungs. Go away and let the scorpions of ambition gnaw your brain like Nimrod's. Go back, so that a dog may not be the lowest on the filthy earth." Then sadly, "Go away, so that the rose garden of brave men may remain unfilled." Then, angrily, "Go, coward! Descend! Leave this place!"

With his hands, Buddha made a sign to the stones. Then everything—the stones, soil, and grass—began to flow down the slope as fast as lightning, carrying me away. At last, coming to a cliff, I fell into a dark chasm. Tearing my lungs, my throat, and my lips, a hopeless cry— a moaning of agony and sadness—poured out of me. . . .

I opened my eyes. The smiling, soft face and sad eyes of the Mirror Dede were before me. He gave me the cup in his hand, and I drank. He held up the unsweetened coffee he had just made. "My son, it's not easy to ascend the Hill of Nothingness. It's not easy. . . ." Unable to control myself, I prostrated myself at his feet and asked for permission to visit him the following day

"Give me your word not to tell the adventures we share to anyone else as long as I remain in this country " I gave him my word, and he gave me permission to return

CHAPTER THREE

The Second Day: The Field of Justice

O blessed light, end oppression.
Zarathustra

I left the cemetery and returned home. My mother was astonished, for she was accustomed to seeing me return drunk every night and usually not until the early hours of morning. After I assured her I wasn't ill, she left me alone. I passed time thinking about my dreams and soon fell asleep.

Early the next day I went to the bazaar and bought a few essentials to bring to the Mirror Dede—some cooking pots, plates, dishes, spoons, a brazier, and some cooking fat, rice, and coffee. Then I proceeded to the cemetery where I found him already seated in front of his hut. He wouldn't accept the presents I had brought but simply prepared some coffee. After resting a while, we drank our coffee, and the Mirror Dede took his ney in hand. He blew upon it as he had done on the previous day, and then softly sang:

These events and phenomena, this universe,
is without real luck or constancy.
Where is Eve or Adam?
Where is your wisdom, O Dede?

The moment is this moment is this moment!
The moment is this moment is this moment!

Remembering the past
brings injustice, pain, and grief.
Don't interest yourself in fate.
No one remains; everything disintegrates.

The moment is this moment is this moment!
The moment is this moment is this moment!

For a seeker like yourself,
are troubles and worries not burdens?
Don't be concerned about the body;
don't fret about the future.

The moment is this moment is this moment!
The moment is this moment is this moment!

In this life there is no fidelity.
Every day brings suffering or difficulties.
O you who long for pleasure and for peace,
don't waste your life away.

The moment is this moment is this moment!
The moment is this moment is this moment!

Who knew he was a black horse?
The one who did not know was a fool.
His aim was a moment;
the rest is trouble and anxiety.

The moment is this moment is this moment!
The moment is this moment is this moment!

After a short while the ney's voice softened to a pleasing whisper, I fell asleep. . . .

I awoke within the city of Balkh just as a woman who appeared to be my wife was entering the room. She spoke to me in a language which seemed to be a combination of Persian and Sanskrit. Strange as it may seem, I could comprehend her language perfectly, for I was a man comprised of two persons: I was both "I" and a Persian who had lived thousands of years ago. The woman said, "You're late. You should get dressed so you can watch the holiday festivities."

After eating a hearty breakfast, I put on a long shirt and belt; then placing a shawl over my back and a conical hat upon my head, I went out onto the crowded street. Everyone was walking hurriedly, so I followed along through the streets until we came to an open field in which thousands of people had gathered. A large tent stood at the center of the open space.

I didn't know why I had come nor what was going to happen, so I asked someone nearby. He answered me: "Beginning today, for forty days there will be great festivities. The town criers will soon be calling to invite everyone for the examination. One by one each of us will go before Zarathustra. Whoever can speak the truth will be privileged to witness the spectacle of truth, and upon his forehead there will be drawn the line of happiness. Whoever cannot speak the truth will be deprived of it, and upon his forehead the line of ill fortune will be drawn. If, however, he later manifests some good action or a work of beauty, the line will disappear, and his family, relatives, and friends will then rejoice."

As I was totally ignorant, I felt that naturally I would fail; the line of unhappiness would be drawn upon my forehead. I regretted that I had come and decided to return home. When I told this to the man who had informed me, he said, "Never, never go away! The mark of unhappiness is drawn on the foreheads of those who don't come, as well as those who fail." Just as I had decided that I might as well attempt the test, the criers began to call, and in single file, everyone began to approach the tent. My place in line wasn't far from the front, so within an hour I had reached the entrance. A doorkeeper admitted us one at a time; my turn soon came, and I went inside. With a golden crown upon his head and clothed in an exquisite caftan, Zarathustra sat upon a high throne. Around him about forty elders stood with hands held respectfully on their chests. I was paralyzed by the greatness of the assembly, and began to pray inwardly that I might not be disgraced or cast aside for my ignorance.

Zarathustra spoke, "Where do you come from?"

Words came from my heart, "From God whose causes, inner meanings, and wisdom cannot be known and inquired about."

"Why were you sent?"

"God wanted to separate the holy light and the darkness, to be just with the blessed light and to alleviate the darkness. He called his holy light "I" and the darkness "other than I.""

"What are God's holy light and darkness?"

"The holy light is Hormuz[1]; the darkness is Ahriman."

"Which one of them is dominant?"

"Now both are equal. Neither Hormuz can be dominant over Ahriman nor Ahriman dominant over Hormuz."

"What is this great confusion and disorder? What will be in the end?"

"Hormuz will be victorious over Ahriman; the universe will be completely blessed light."

"What will be later?"

"God will say, 'I am all,' 'all is I' and will not say 'apart from me.'"

"Who are you, to whom do you belong?"

"I belong to the blessed light. I belong to Hormuz."

Zarathustra raised his hands and spoke, "May God transform you into blessed light."

A vertical green line suddenly appeared between my eyebrows; the elders prayed with Zarathustra, "May God bless you; may God bless you."

As I left the tent, people who saw the green line on my forehead

1. Hormuz, Ahriman: In the Zoroastrian religion, Ahura Mazda is the Supreme Lord. The forces of good are personified in the power of the holy light—Hormuz. The forces of evil are personified in the power of darkness—Ahriman.

parted ranks respectfully to allow me to pass. I was given a friend to guide me. We mounted horses that had been held ready for us and rode off toward the emerald hills visible in the East. After traveling for a few hours, we arrived at a kind of caravanserai² where we spent the rest of the day.

When we arose the next morning, my guide led me to a room where he told me, "You'll be engaging in a very difficult battle. Do you have any skill in the use of weapons like the sword, the shield, or the mace?" The room which we had just entered was filled with weapons of all sorts. My guide helped me to put on a suit of armor and then pointed to an iron club that he wished me to try. I felt an unfamiliar power and skill arise within me and soon won his approval in ironclub and sword games.

After each of us chose a set of the most perfect weapons to take with us, we mounted our winged steeds and flew till evening when we arrived at the foot of a frightful mountain. It was so high that its peak was not even visible, as though it had pierced the skies and disappeared into the unknown. When I inquired, my guide informed me that this was "The Pinnacle." After passing the night at the foot of the mountain, we rose with the sun, mounted our horses, and flew toward the peak at a speed beyond thought. As we arrived our eyes beheld an incredible panorama, never before seen by man. Before us lay an open field as wide as the world. The left half was so dark that in comparison the darkest nights could be called "bright," while the right half was so bright that in comparison clear sunlight might be called "dim." We were astonished that, like our inner knowing, our eyes could withstand this brightness. It burned our sight, enabling us to see—as if it were daylight—into every corner of the intense darkness which reminded me of Hell.

Innumerable people gathered on this field which resembled the place of the Last Judgment. Some were on the right side in the sea of light, and some were on the left in the sea of darkness. In between, the space was empty. Two large thrones had been placed at the end of this emptiness. Hormuz was sitting on the one which faced the light,

2. caravanserai: A place of shelter for caravan travelers with stabling areas for animals.

and the unique brightness radiating from his face was apparent even in that glittering field. Ahriman sat on the throne which stood at the edge of darkness; his filthy face was uglier than the most terrible of monsters. There was, however, a throne hovering between the thrones of Hormuz and Ahriman. Hanging in the sky, it lent a strange grandeur to the unusual sights below. We moved through the open area, straight to the side of Hormuz, joining the ranks there.

After a while an incomprehensible noise began. From every mouth came the words, "Look, look! . . . The order of Izid[3] descended to the earth!" On the heavenly throne stood an angel, the personification of Beauty, who held in its hand a sphere, the east of which was brilliant with light and the west of which was dark. There was such a balance between the light and the darkness that no flow occurred from the blessed light to the side veiled in darkness nor from the dark side towards the blessed light. The crowds of people on the right below cried, "Izid, God! Remove the darkness!" and those on the side of Ahriman were crying, "O veil of darkness! Show the truth!" Wondrously, with a luminous face and sweet voice able to penetrate every ear, the beauty hovering above announced, "This is the field of justice and examination."

Immediately, everyone became quiet, and both sides humbly began to pray. Amid the deep silence, Hormuz stood and delivered this speech:

"O Mankind! God created you so that you might become holy light like Himself. He preferred you to all creatures; He granted you all kinds of favors; yet when you were holy light, He combined you with darkness. When you were spirit, He combined you with the corpse so that you might abolish the darkness He hates with the holy light He loves. O, son of Adam! I am the holy light. Come to me. Be mine. Become me. Be virtuous with the beauties demanded by the spirit. Fear God; prefer your own true self to your ego.[4] Throw away the ugly attributes of darkness: resentment, jealousy, insincerity, anger,

3. Izid: Izid represents the Supreme Lord. See note #1
4. ego: *al-nafs al-ammarah*, the unruly animal self, the compulsive self, the coarsest of the stages of the soul. The word *nafs* is derived from the word for breath. As the *nafs*—the self or soul—develops and transforms, it passes through six other stages:

enmity, ambition, pride, and envy. In every circumstance, thank God. Be content with whatever He gives. Go out from this place of examination as holy light so that the universe of blessed light may be your eternal abode."

Hormuz sat down. Ahriman stood and spoke:

"O, mankind! Open your eyes . . . contemplate well the needs of your nature. Don't follow these poetic words; they are lies. Don't let your life slip away for nothing. Laugh; entertain yourself and enjoy yourself; eat and drink. There are only two true motivations in life: pride and desire. The rest are false. The ego directs humankind toward these two; act accordingly. Prefer your ego to everything else. Never mind if thousands of people are dying at the cost of a single pleasure of yours. This is the necessity of your nature, of all nature as well. A small bird eats the insects; bigger birds eat smaller ones. Sometimes hunger or cold destroys the big birds. An insect eats seeds; soon that insect becomes the food of another animal who is then swallowed by yet another. Sheep eat the grass, and you eat the sheep. This universe is based on appetite and mutual destruction. Every being is the constant enemy of another. Even those who are saved from the greedy teeth of some larger creature one day will become bait swallowed by mesmerizing death. . . . This is the truth. Don't obey the principles given you. Don't ever acknowledge any existence other than your own ego, nor any aim other than your own pleasure."

After this, Hormuz slowly stood up:

"O men! Don't listen to this low creature, this outcast giant Ahriman. His words are lies. True service in God's name is a great

---

·al-nafs al-lawwamah, the self of conscience, the struggling moral self;

·al-nafs al-mulhima, the inspired self; by the inspiration of spiritual knowledge one is able to know right from wrong and follow one's enlightened conscience;

·al-nafs al-mutma'innah, the tranquil soul that enjoys relationship with the Divine;

·al-nafs al-radiyyah, the satisfied soul, the submissive soul in harmony with Reality;

·al-nafs al-mardiyyah, the totally submissive soul lost in God, a soul which totally identifies with Divine will;

·al-nafs al-zakiyyah, the completely purified or perfected soul.

pleasure compared to the false satisfactions of pride. There are spiritual pleasures compared to which sexual pleasures seem undesirable. The carnal spirit, the ego about which Ahriman spoke, is an instinct which belongs to animals. The ego of man must be balanced with wisdom. Although man is a flower that has grown in the garden of nature, he is a different sort of flower with a unique spirit-enlivening fragrance. This is wisdom. Most of the laws that govern the animal kingdom are altered in their application to man. Don't be deceived."

Enraged, Ahriman called out, "Hormuz is lying! He wants you weak and helpless, submissive under some concocted laws and fantastic utopian principles. He wants to make you even more powerless and subservient than the lowest of animals. He wants to deprive you of your most simple pleasures. Don't listen. Don't listen to Hormuz, the lackey of God."

Accusing each other of being liars, they began to attack each other, but the personification of beauty above them extended the sphere in her hand and called to them: "The time hasn't yet come. Don't struggle in vain; the battle will be between those who follow you."

Then Hormuz turned and called, "Those who love me, let them come out into the open." Ahriman echoed him.

Together with my guide, I moved into the ranks of the combatants on the right side where we were greeted with respect. We passed the night in their camp.

The next morning the drums rolled, and a warrior from Ahriman's side came forward, asking for a challenger. A warrior from our side went forward to meet him. After a short struggle, he was defeated, and another warrior was sent forth. Victory passed back and forth as twenty warriors fell. Each day many died as the battle continued.

On the seventh day, a champion from our side fought until nightfall, killing fifty of Ahriman's followers. Each time one of Ahriman's heroes fell, the drums of "good news" were beaten and cries of "May God be praised" rose to the skies; there was great celebration among us. That night though, our spies informed us that the following day a great hero of Ahriman's, who had never been defeated, would come onto the field. Everyone became apprehensive.

My guide and I went to visit the tent of one of the spies, where we stayed and talked for a long while. We learned that it was the demon Hypocrisy who would come forward the next day. It was said that this demon had been sentenced to live until the Last Judgment, that he was impossible to kill. This was why everyone was so agitated and concerned. I, too, was curious and anxious and all through the night dreamed of strange battles.

When morning came, accompanied by drumbeats, Hypocrisy rode onto the field upon a huge, steel-armored horse. An awesome warrior, he rode around the battlefield shouting, "Where is my opponent? I am that wrestler whose sharp sword has split so many heads in two. I am the brave one whose arrow has pierced so many powerful chests. Is there anyone who will challenge me? The one who is tired of his soul or depressed! Let him come!"

Though knowing that whoever fell into the hands of Hypocrisy would soon die, a warrior loyal to Hormuz came forward. It wasn't long before he succumbed. One after the other, thirty men came forward and were slaughtered. For the following three days, Hypocrisy ruled the field, killing thirty or forty warriors each day. On the evening of the third day, I noticed a change in the atmosphere among our ranks; the sadness coloring peoples faces had disappeared, replaced now by the light of hope. When I asked my guide about this, he answered, "Tomorrow, one of the most beloved servants, the hero Affection, will be coming forward to fight. It has become clear that no one else can defeat this damned Hypocrisy. Tonight, one of Hormuz's representatives, Progress, will come to speak to us."

At midnight the elder, Progress, came. He encouraged everyone to sacrifice their lives for the sake of Right and Truth, and in closing, he recited a prayer.

The following morning, the demon Hypocrisy reappeared. Laughing sarcastically, he shouted, "Isn't there anyone who is tired of his life today? Why is the field left empty?"

Amid much acclaim and shouts of "God is most Great!," Affection entered the field from Hormuz's side. As soon as Hypocrisy saw the hero Affection, his eyes reddened with rage. "I have been waiting for you for three days. So at last you have appeared. Prepare to die!"

The warrior Affection uttered a clear and beautiful cry, calling, "He who knows, let him know me. . . . He who doesn't know, let him know that I am the hero Affection. Like a lion, I tear hearts to pieces and sever heads. You, Hypocrisy, know that when I appear, I always lay you to waste unmercifully. Enough now. Be ready for your death!"

Hypocrisy declared, "Yes, you have beaten me before, but this time I am sure I will destroy you."

"Never, for Affection always will triumph over Hypocrisy."

The attack began; sparks flew as sword struck shield and was parried. When evening fell there was still no clear victory. Not until the third day, when the sun was exactly at mid-heaven, did the lion Affection strike down Hypocrisy. The joyous cries of the followers of Hormuz rose to the skies, while the rage of Ahriman's followers shook the world. By that evening, Affection had defeated thirty more combatants, and for seven days no one could resist him.

In the evening of the seventh day, our spies informed us that yet another renowned warrior of Ahriman would be sent forth the next morning. Even before the rising of the sun, we heard sounds of the arrival of this new foe. A giant of a man, he inspired great awe as he rode onto the field upon a yellow camel, brandishing an iron club as big as a man's head. As he circled the field, he called out, "Friends of Hormuz, which of you is going to challenge me? I am Wrath. Very few survive battle with me."

The hero Affection came out to meet Wrath. Day after day they fought until the afternoon of the third day when Wrath struck Affection to the ground. While Affection yet lived, without any pity for this beautiful hero, Wrath tore his body into pieces with his teeth, and cast Affection's heart in front of Ahriman. Wrath declared, "Let the heart of Affection, one of the greatest of our enemies, be tred upon by your feet." This tragic death wounded our hearts greatly, but the followers of Ahriman exulted.

Exactly thirty-eight days had passed since this strange festival had begun, and no one from our side had yet been able to defeat Wrath. Darkness had spread to enshroud the right side of the sphere in the hand of the mysterious beauty above Hormuz and Ahriman. Victory appeared imminent for Ahriman's forces.

The elder, Progress, came past us. He told us that only the warrior Wisdom could defeat Wrath and that Hormuz had ordered him to come onto the field the next day. As only two days of the festival remained, we were all asked to offer special prayers that night. When we returned to our tent, my guide looked at me earnestly,"Do you know who Wisdom is?"

"No," I replied.

"You are Wisdom. Tonight is not the time for sleep, for tomorrow you will fight Wrath, Ahriman's second fiercest warrior. We'll pass the rest of the night in sword training and prayer."

I froze on the spot, astonished. I had never imagined that such a task would be given to me. I had not known my name was "Wisdom." Nonetheless, I began to feel a surge of determination and power within myself as I came to understand that I would soon be engaging in holy battle with Wrath. Until morning, I prayed sincerely, asking not to be defeated and for Wrath not to overcome the holy light. My guide instructed me in methods of attack. When it was time for morning prayer, I put on my armor, and my guide helped me to wrap my woven armor belt. Then with tears in his eyes he kissed me on the forehead and offered a final prayer. With the rising of the sun, I mounted my horse and readied myself. When Wrath appeared, I went forth. He asked my name:

"The warrior Wisdom," I replied.

Wrath jeered, "O poor man! Can an exhausted, old fool like you ever fight with a roaring lion like me? You're a harmless imbecile. Flee while you can! It is beneath me to even shed your blood."

I answered, "I know you can never defeat me. Do you trust your simple brain? Don't you realize that if I weren't able to defeat you, I would not have been sent to challenge you? Don't say another word; get ready to die!"

Wrath was angry now, "You must be drunk, you're talking such rubbish. Here I am; defend yourself if you can!" he yelled and began attacking me.

I had to be quite swift in order to save myself from the deadly blows of this awesome giant, but happily I was as light as a bird and could leap through the air. We fought until evening. He could not catch me even with a single blow, but I was unable to strike him either. After a brief rest, my guide and I passed the following night in prayer. Towards morning, he gave me further advice, and when morning arrived, I went out onto the field again.

Filled with rage, spinning around me like a top, Wrath yelled as he positioned himself to strike, "Yesterday you escaped from my hands, but today you won't."

According to the instructions my guide had given me, I asked him, "What's that you have on your head?" He moved his hand to his head and immediately I inserted my sword through his armpit where there was a gap in his armor; it pierced right to his heart. With a terrible cry, he fell, and blood spewed from his mouth.

Angry cries rose from the side of Ahriman, "Wisdom struck Wrath unfairly," they complained.

Yet the sphere in the hand of the mysterious one began filling with blessed light and the joyful cries from our side vibrated in the air. I continued killing many enemies that morning until at noon a warrior whose face was hidden came in front of me. As he appeared, riding a white elephant, Ahriman's face trembled with an evil joy and Hormuz's face grew ashen. Turning to the mysterious one above, Hormuz asked, "Izid! Izid! Do you intend to destroy the holy light? Mercy! . . . Mercy!"

The representative of God answered, "It is Ahriman's right. What can I do? He has the right to bring forth whomever he likes."

Ahriman laughed, and Hormuz bowed his head sadly. "The order is yours," he said.

Like everyone else, I overheard this conversation indicating that my time of victory had ended. The warrior on the elephant rode proudly around the field and then gave a cry that shook us like thunder.

"You who out of ignorance deny my power! Know that I am Ego, the warrior of warriors and the hero of heroes. There has never been

31

anyone whom I could not defeat in one to one combat. I can change into five thousand forms; I have more than a thousand weapons." Turning to me, he continued, "O, poor Wisdom! Come, surrender your will; let me use you well. You are a foolish, weak creature, worth less than a fly in my hand. But though I don't know why, I like you. Perhaps because you have served me, too. Come, give up your sword and be saved."

I gathered my courage and stood firm.

"O Wisdom! Look at the weapons I have. Your defenses—meekness, knowledge, contentment, humbleness, patience—and all the tricks your guide has taught you have no effect on me. Against each one of them, I have endless exhausting parries: resentment, rage, deceit, hatred, and lust. Come, have pity on yourself!" he admonished me.

I hesitated.

Ego continued his attempt to dissuade me. "O helpless one! What are you thinking!? Your thrusts can have no effect on me. I could annihilate you in a moment."

Standing firm in my own knowledge, I refused to be intimidated but moved determinedly into battle. I tried every blow that I knew but had no success. Ego laughed at my dilemma. Finally, I prepared to make my final attack, called "powerful determination and will" which I knew to be the most effective. I moved to position myself to the left side of Ego.

Ego, recognizing my intent, said, "So! . . . You still want to annihilate me, eh! We'll see." And just when I was about to insert my sword into his chest, this warrior removed the veil over his face. An incredible beauty dazzled my eyes, and the sword fell from my hand. Ego caught me by my belt and pulled me onto the elephant, carrying me into the presence of Ahriman.

"O Ahriman! I didn't kill Wisdom; I captured him. Let him peel onions in our kitchen, a service that would suit him well."

Ahriman burst into laughter. Hormuz wept. The blessed light was gradually disappearing from the ball in the hand of the mysterious one. It seemed that Ahriman's forces had won. They cried out, "The darkness! The darkness! The essence is darkness! We are victorious!"

Our side entreated, "Creator, Creator! O Light of Light! Don't remove your Light!" and Hormuz prostrated himself in front of the mysterious being of Blessed Light and Beauty.

"Unique Izid! Help, help us, we implore you! For God's sake!" he begged.

Hormuz remained with head bowed; Ahriman raised his head towards the sky. The darkness had invaded the sphere to such an extent that only a tiny, nearly imperceptible, light spot remained at its edge. But at that moment, we began to hear someone singing approach us from very far away. The voice was as pleasant as it was manly. At last from deep within the darkness, a mounted warrior appeared from whose face such a light radiated that his surroundings became illuminated, enabling him to be seen. Riding on a four-footed dragon with horned forehead and green wings, this warrior emanated the essence of beauty. His curly, almost chestnut hair, which occasionally shone with a deep red brilliance, reached to his shoulders. He wore green silk clothing and, upon his head, a crown sparkled with precious stones. He continued to sing, and we listened timidly:

> I am he before whose crushing power
> the universe is trembling.
> I am he whose strength rules every living creature.
> I am he before whom everyone surrenders.
> Mankind bows at the dust of my feet.
> I am he who is unique among the virtues of humanity.
> My servants are the brave.
> I am he who judges all people equally.
> For me, kings and beggars are the same.
> In short, I am the sword of God's majesty.
> I am Love;
> My power causes the universe to quake.

This sweet voice engendered gaiety in both ranks. It was strange that Ahriman's forces were enjoying his singing as much as we were. The closer this hero, Love, came to us, the brighter became the sphere in the hand of the mysterious being of Light above us. Light was removing the darkness. When Love came to the center of the field, the sphere became completely luminous, and the darkness departed from the universe. Ego and servant "I" were on the field. Love directed his dragon towards us. With a very gentle and easy manner, he spoke, "Carnal Spirit! Are you also going to challenge me?"

Ego bowed, dismounted from the elephant, and knelt down before Love, declaring, "As you are for everyone else, you are also my master and my benefactor. I declare my helplessness and here prostrate myself in front of you."

Love freed me, laughing, "All right, great Wisdom, relax!"

Only Love was left on the field. He got down off his dragon and, with hands crossed over his chest, began walking with slow, harmoniously measured steps toward the mysterious one of the Blessed Light. When there were but three steps remaining, he spoke, "O Light of Beauty, I am your servant," and he prostrated himself in worship.

He then spoke to Hormuz, "O, Hormuz! O, Blessed Light! Peace be upon you that the darkness was known with you!"

Then to Ahriman he said, "O, Ahriman! O, Veil of Darkness! Peace be upon you that the worth of the Blessed Light was known with you!"

Then he withdrew to the center of the field and raised his hands to the sky. Hormuz and Ahriman had come down from their thrones and shaken hands and were now standing side by side. On each side people were coming forward to kiss their master's hand. The mysterious one of the Blessed Light surveyed this scene, smiling. I kissed the hand of Hormuz and looked into his face. What did I see!? From astonishment, I cried aloud. . . .

When I opened my eyes, I saw the smiling face of the Mirror.

CHAPTER FOUR

The Third Day: The Eternal Cycle

Everlasting One! Infinite One!
You who are the First! You who are the Last!
You who are the Hidden One!
Hear my voice, Apparent One,
as you heard the voice of Your servant Zachariah!
  Abu'l-Hasan Ali ash-Shadhili

*A*gain today, I was transported by the sound of the ney into another world. I saw myself as a boy of twelve living with my family in a very beautiful house on a gracious street in a large city. The bright morning sun had just begun to illuminate my room.

I was about to get out of bed when the door opened. A servant entered and informed me that my father was waiting, so I arose and followed him. We entered a large room.

My father, an old man of about a hundred and ten, spoke in Sanskrit: "My son, you are twelve-years-old now, and the time has come for you to learn about yourself and the universe. I am pleased that you have reached the age of wisdom. Soon I will take you to our greatest master, but first we will hold a celebration for three days and nights. After serving our guests, you will be introduced to the assistant master who will be your guide."

An extravagant celebration was prepared. On the first day, all the Brahmans and high-ranking officers were invited; on the second day, the soldiers and merchants; and on the third, the poor. Each day, I served the guests. At the end of the third day, an eighty-year-old fakir became my guide.

Early the next morning, my father sent us on our way. My guide rode a donkey, but I walked behind him. He told me, "My son, you will go on foot so that you may learn to appreciate the price of wisdom. Nothing is appreciated unless you sacrifice for it."

During those first days I suffered quite a bit, but gradually I adapted. Finally, after a forty-day journey, we stopped in front of a hut to rest. My guide took my hand and led me inside. The hut was empty except for a single cup filled with water. Turning me to the East, he placed the cup in front of me, cautioned me to gaze upon it steadily, and prayed: "O Brahma! O First and Pure Existence! O Great Light! Reveal the stages of the body and the phases of spirit!" He murmured some other words I couldn't understand and then rose and left the hut, closing the door behind him. Everything became quite dark except for the translucent glow of the water in the cup before me. Obeying my guide's warning, I looked at it continuously. After a while I began to hear a sound but could not determine its source. Was it a moaning voice, an inspiration, or a delusion? I couldn't even distinguish which language was being used, but somehow, in the vibration of the sound itself, I could hear and understand the following poem:

O visitor to the gathering of the body,
understand what the secret of phenomena is.
No limitation lives in the moment of Unity,
whatever you say His name is.
Within everything is that hidden point.
Sometimes It is ether, sometimes the universe.
The cup of life and death belongs to It.

At times the sun, at times the moon;

At times the rain, at times the cloud.
It is the fire; It is the flame.
It is the night; It is the dawn.

At times the stone, at times the plant;
at times the lion, at times the ant.
It is spirit; It is the corpse.
It is life; It is death.

Through the cycle It will be nothingness perfected.
He finds Himself in himself.
He becomes a dot when He is the absolute.
It was Adam, the honor and manifestation of God.

The water in the cup gradually lost its brilliance, and the darkness also disappeared. I couldn't see anything, but then as I persisted in focusing my eyes on the cup, a strange scene began to unfold. Though I could distinguish nothing but darkness, somehow I was seeing. An infinite field stretched out before me. In one moment I visited places that were millions of centuries away; yet I did not leave the spot where I was. This infinite majesty shattered feelings and perceptions as it grew brighter and brighter, but then it also disappeared. Now within this expansive feeling, indistinguishably mine or not mine, I lost myself. For a moment, I became nothing.

After some time, I again began to discern an infinite field. An indescribable feeling stirred me. It was as if within myself I had gathered this infinity which at the same time included me. I don't know how long this state lasted, but after a while I began to feel a density within myself, and something which had been unseen came out into the open. Essentially, nothing was yet apparent—no light, no darkness, not a thing—nothing! Yet still I felt there was something. Then all at once, this non-thing burst magically into light. At first it was such a weak light that it trembled like the beats of my heart. This subtle presence began to emerge, resembling Israfil's[1] call to prayer, a song of meaning without words:

1. Israfil: one of the four archangels—Gabriel, Azrail, Michael, and Israfil.

37

God is most great, God is most great!
O secret of existence that is nonexistence!
You are well-known, but You are not known.
You are apparent, but You are not seen.

Within this moment, hours, years, millions of centuries passed through my experience. Exhausted, I felt as though I had closed my eyes, because for a moment I wasn't seeing anything. But when I opened my eyes wider, I beheld a universe which extended infinitely and yet was small enough to fit into the palm of my hand. During this vision, one part of the universe—a sphere completely covered with water—caught my attention.

As I gazed at the water, an incomprehensible attraction drew me to it; I entered it. It was warm. Right away I saw that I was now among millions of strange, amorphous creatures.

Though I tried to save myself from being identified with their existence, I failed. As they shifted into a mass of millions of rooms, I found myself living within them. And due to some indistinct wish to remain, I lingered for millions of years. Even though little by little strange differences evolved, I was disturbed by the feeling of being imprisoned by their limitation, being removed from any thoughts, perceptions, or feelings.

These little creatures under my control began to take on myriad forms, and with the passage of thousands of centuries, which was like a day for me, each revealed some new change. But, imprisoned by the water, I grew tired of the strange sights and the deafness of my ears. At last a time came when I found myself not only in the sea but within the bodies of many little land animals as well.

The feeling of fresh air entering my lungs filled me with such joy that I ran about, playing within millions of those bodies. A vague but nonetheless real feeling of love flowed into these bodies of mine. Although I didn't really comprehend all that I was experiencing, somehow their existence was coincident with mine, and I enjoyed all the forms which were not harmful to me. Each moment, some of my bodies remained motionless; some changed forms; some became minerals; while at the same time, millions more emerged into being. There was no apparent reason that these creatures formed; it wasn't due to a uniting of bodies, but in a moment of love, two bodies would disappear in a strange ecstasy. As I had neither a completely male nor completely female body—each of my bodies having the characteristics of both sexes—I was at times a father, at times a mother, and sometimes both father and mother. As time passed, the bodies under my protection multiplied and became so varied that some now appeared totally different in form from the others. Some remained small and primitive and impossible to see. Others flew through the air or crawled upon the ground. Some were quite magnificent; others were gentle and wise. There were those who were eager to eat others, for some were strong while others were weak. After a while, decaying corpses were strewn everywhere as rivalry and exploitation became the rule among them.

Time passed; what happened?

One day, I found myself moaning with pain. I felt imprisoned in a corpse while at the same time it seemed that all the secrets given temporarily to each particle of the universe were gathering one by one within that single body. A spaceless, colorless breath of meaning filled me. I had turned to the East and was facing the horizon which seemed about to explode. It was as if every particle were greeting me with "Peace be upon you," and everywhere was the scent of ambergris. My whole existence trembled under the effect of an intuition of friendship. I was conscious of myself and was also conscious that I was seeing and behaving as though I knew everything. Rapture filled me, and in my heart arose the meaning of "Praise the Lord." A voice from the invisible worlds was proclaiming to the whole universe:

Now the perception of the sun
    is born into the universe.
The mind of Adam is the place of equality.
The ruby glittering in the night
    is the Blessed Light of God.
O angels! Bow down before Adam.

All universes and beings contained within them trembled in response to this magnificent command. Every creature bowed before man. Every particle, in its own language, spoke to me:

Greetings. . . .
Greetings, light of the secret of the body!
Greetings, origin of all phenomena!
Greetings, source of knowledge and wisdom!
Greetings, manifestation of the gift of the body!
You were the aim of the universe, you!
O intellect! We are your mirror.
You are the dot; we are your signs.
You are the place of prostration;
the divine orientation!

I opened my eyes. . . .
The sad glance of the Mirror Dede was focused on me. Like children who begin to tell their dreams when they awaken, I spoke, "All of them prostrated in worship."

"Yes," the Mirror Dede replied, "all except the devil—the pride within your own ego!"

CHAPTER FIVE

The Fourth Day:
The Assembling Place of the Wise

O my Lord in whom I trust, I declare that You are beyond all attributes that can be known. We have not known You as You should be known. We are not worthy of such knowledge.

Muhammad (Peace and Blessings upon him)

*T*oday, as before, I had gone to the hut of the great Mirror. After I ate my daily portion, rather than sitting with me in front of the hut, the Mirror Dede led me to a remote spot in the cemetery, far from the noise of the street. Pointing to a large gravestone, he told me, "Go and lie down on that grave. The marvelous turban adorning it would make you think this person was one of the greatest scholars of his time." Smiling, he continued, "Go, learn from the spirituality of such a wise one!"

I lay down on the grave as he suggested. The turban took on myriad forms in my mind, until after a few minutes I fell asleep while listening to the sad moanings of the ney. . . .

I saw myself lying on a bed in a pitch-dark room. While darkness enveloped me, I waited. I was just noticing that the darkness was disturbing me and was beginning to try to figure out where I was, when the door of the room opened. Someone entered and spoke, "Have you awakened, my son?"

Through the darkness I was unable to see who the person was that had entered; yet with some new sense, I was able to discern that it seemed to be my father. Since my father had died some time ago, I was astonished to be called "my son" by this man. Again he spoke, "My son, have you awakened?"

"Yes," I replied, "but are you really my father?"

With a bewildered voice, he asked, "My son, are you going mad?"

"No," I answered, "but since my father died . . ."

"Oh no!" he interrupted. "My son has been smitten by jinns.[1] My boy, you're talking nonsense."

Right away I pulled myself together, for the mad are not often treated very pleasantly. Out of fear I quickly tried to correct my mistake "Father, I was just joking, but would you please ask someone to bring in a lamp or a candle; it's dark as hell in here."

The poor man lamented, "My son must be going crazy! When the eternal sun has risen and the universe is filled with light, he insists that it is dark. O my son, I don't feel well."

Though the room was absolutely dark, my father kept insisting that it was broad daylight. I was beginning to believe that this man, claiming to be my father, was really the one who was crazy. In order to test him without making him angry, I said, "Daddy, really the sun has risen; this is true, but perhaps the windows are shuttered, and that is why the light is not getting through."

"Good Lord!" he exclaimed. "Our boy is surely losing his mind. My son, can anything stop the light of the sun? Are you mad? What is happening?"

"With this last response of his, I began to wonder if I had awakened in an insane asylum. After a while a woman claiming to be my mother, accompanied by aunts and uncles and various other supposed relatives, entered the room. With great anxiety, my father informed them I was on the verge of madness. Crowding around me, my rela-

1. jinns (anglicized: "genie"): elemental spirits whose being is of fire and air. Jinns are capable of assuming many different forms and are said to be responsible for much mischief affecting human beings, but like humans they are also subject to final judgment by God.

tives prodded me with silly questions. I realized that no matter what I said, they would conclude that I was crazy, so I decided to keep silent. My new father sat weeping next to me. I was petrified, unsure what to do or say. Then I remembered a box of matches in my pocket, took it out, and struck one. What I saw was so strange I burst out laughing and almost rolled off the bed. In place of eyes these people had somethng like shallots instead. No wonder they didn't realize it was dark. All these helpless creatures lacked the finest and most essential of our five senses; they had no eyes with which to see.

Immediately everyone in the room reacted to my laughter in an extraordinary, disturbing way. All of my relatives, including my supposed father and mother, suddenly dropped down on all fours and began jumping earnestly around the room. After a short while my father stopped and came to my side. Taking my hand, he kissed it and proclaimed: "O Yellow Devil of the White Demon. We give thanks to the Sovereign Power for your arrival! For a thousand years the whole universe has been awaiting you. At last the great miracle has occurred; you have been born from my generation. At last, you've manifested the sound for which we have been waiting so long. I must announce this glorious news to all the scarlet devils that they may come and kiss your hand. Let everyone be informed!"

I had managed to fabricate a lamp with some olive oil I found and was looking for something to eat when the king and numerous illustrious ministers and scholars poured into our house. After giving me the strange title, "His Majesty, the Yellow Devil of the White Demon," everyone bowed before me with great respect. The good news that the Yellow Devil had appeared was being proclaimed throughout the city. They consecrated the largest and most beautiful palace in the country for my use and gave me hundreds of servants to care for all my needs.

Little by little, I began to make a study of these strange people. I discovered that they were not completely blind. They were unable to see in the usual way that we receive light; they were in continual darkness, but they had their own strange sense of seeing. Their cities had been beautifully built, and they had accomplished astonishing works in many areas of the arts. Literature, philosophy, and theology were especially important to them, and within their countless universities there were many famous scholars and professors.

One day, I attended the graduation exams of the school of theology. The professors and students were thrilled to have me present. The chancellor declared that all science, cultural attainment, and truth belong only to the Yellow Devil, and that the university would ask me to assess and confirm all the knowledge which they had acquired. They then asked my permission to begin the examination.

First, questions were asked of an eminent student called "Bibi." Seated in the first row, he began speaking about the creation of the universe: "According to the words of the scholar Tata, who lived many years ago, the White Demon lived in a golden heaven, together with the purple devils, fifteen thousand years ago."

Suddenly someone interrupted: "For three thousand years you have been insisting on this erroneous idea! The devils who were together with the White Demon were not purple; they were light blue."

The chancellor then spoke: "Sir, the student is taking an oral exam; objections are not permitted. Some other time in the presence of His Majesty, the Yellow Devil, you may yourself be examined by our scholars."

It became clear that the one who had interrupted was the famous scholar Tantan. For some time he had tried to disseminate new ideas that were contrary to established public opinions, but he had been silenced by the government. Now he had come to the examination to take advantage of my presence in order to declare his objections.

The student being examined continued: "Though the purple devils were extremely obedient to the White Demon, they were very foolish, so the White Demon decided to bring forth a more intelligent creature. Sweeping the sky, he made an open space with eight corners. Then he spat into the sky, and a great sea formed. He placed the ground upon the sea, and this was the beginning of our universe. But the water of the sea was frozen, and the world was filled with ice, so the White Demon made a huge cauldron and hung it over the universe. He filled the cauldron with his spit and boiled it with his breath. The universe grew warmer. He took some of the purple devils and chipped them smaller. He made a hole in each one, inflated them, and then gave them their freedom; these were our first ancestors."

Again the voice of Tantan was heard: "The cauldron! The cauldron! Everyone is talking about a cauldron! How many handles does this cauldron have? By how many handles is it hung? *From what* does it hang? You ignorant people! Not one of you apprehends this secret!"

Both sides began shouting. With the approval of the king, the student's examination was postponed. It was decided that in seven days all the famous scholars of the land would gather to present their ideas before me. I would then decide whose knowledge was correct. The present assembly was adjourned.

At the end of the week, a large assembly met in the main square of the capital city. I had made lamps by filling great pots with olive oil and had them positioned all around the square. The scholars had divided into two opposing groups: the critics, or religious reformers, under the leadership of Tantan, and the traditionalists under the leadership of the scholar Tonton. Tantan and Tonton came forward. Tonton spoke first: "O Tantan, you know it is not permissable to question our established scientific knowledge. This ancient knowledge has been passed down for thousands of years. Let's hear your objections now in the presence of His Majesty the Yellow Devil that we may have an end to this charlatanism."

Tantan answered: "Tonton, I am not objecting to your theories on every point, but you're an enemy of progress. You aren't continuing to investigate or attempting to expand your knowledge. For instance, you say the devils who were with the White Demon were purple."

"That is the tradition."

"Yes, but it's wrong. Even if the devils living in the presence of the White Demon for thousands of years were essentially purple, wouldn't their color fade and become blue from the effect of the White Demon's light? O Tonton, be reasonable!"

"It might be so, but there isn't any evidence."

"How can it not be so? If I leave something solid in front of the fire, it eventually softens. Some solids even melt. Therefore, the purple devils have surely become blue by now."

"As I said before, it might be so."

"You believe that the heat comes from the cauldron hung over the universe."

"That the heat comes to us from the cauldron of the sky is proven by the low temperature of the the night and the contrasting heat of the day and by the seasons."

"How many handles does this sky cauldron have?"

Tonton could not answer this important question.

Tantan spoke again: "So, you are silent! Well, I've discovered the secret. The huge sky cauldron has seven hundred and sixty-eight-and-a-half handles."

My patience was thoroughly exhausted with this nonsense. Naming the sun the "Cauldron of the Sky," and saying it is boiled with breath and held up by seven hundred and sixty-eight-and-a-half handles, and regarding all this as a secret science! I burst out laughing at the absurdity of it all, but because my laughter had been determined to be the divine sound that these people had been awaiting for thousands of years, it was now taken as a sign of approval of Tantan and his theories. Immediately everyone began to worship in that same strange way of jumping about on all fours. Tantan and Tonton and everyone present began jumping madly about. . . .

I woke up still laughing and beheld the smiling face of the Mirror father in front of me. He asked me, "What do you say now about the comparisons of the virtuous and the beauty of scholarly ideas? When compared to the Truth, mankind's science is not unlike the discoveries of Tantan. And that is the way it will be until the end of time, because in seeing truths, the eyes of mankind are about as worthy and reliable as shallots."

CHAPTER SIX

The Fifth Day:
The Place of Grandeur

His throne extends over the heavens and the earth.
and He feels no fatigue in guarding and preserving them,
for He is the Highest and Most Magnificent.
  "The Throne Verse," Qur'an II: 255

*T*oday the sky was overcast, but rather than being oppressive, the air was cool and pleasant. When I arrived, the Mirror Dede was standing outside the hut with a pot of semolina halvah in his hand. I had become accustomed to arriving early in order to lie down for a while in front of the hut. This morning it wasn't long before a strange dream state overtook me. . . .

I saw myself as the muezzin[1] of the Hagia Sophia mosque. Looking at my watch, I realized that it was time for the morning call to prayer, so I climbed the stairs up to the balcony of the minaret. As soon as I had proclaimed, "Allahu Akbar" (God is most Great), a big bird flew towards the minaret and, seizing me with her claw, placed me upon her back and flew away with me.

1. muezzin: the servant of the mosque who five times daily proclaims the call to prayer from the balcony of the minaret of a large mosque, or the doorway of a smaller one. He is chosen for his good character.

When my fear and astonishment had lessened a bit, I was able to look around. While the rising sun brought color to the sky, I watched in awe as the peak of the minaret disappeared far beneath me.

The bird's back was as large as a spacious room. The surface appeared flat, and all kinds of food, clothes, and other things necessary for human comfort were placed about on shelves and in cupboards along both sides. Quite bewildered, I called out, "O Lord! What kind of a bird is this and where is it taking me?"

Hearing my words, the bird turned her head and answered: "I am the famous Phoenix.[2] You needn't be afraid; no harm will come to you. I am the queen of the phoenix; fifty more, loaded with provisions, fly behind me. You will lack nothing."

Sadly, I persisted, "All right, but why did you seize me? Where are you taking me?"

"I was ordered by someone whom I cannot disappoint. I am taking you to watch the universes unfold," she answered.

It somehow seemed inevitable, so I resigned myself to my fate. In any case I had no fear of falling off, for the back of the Phoenix was like a comfortable sofa resting on a floor of feathers and was quite comfortable. As I am a little greedy, I soon began looking in the cupboards for something to eat. I found some biscuits and ate them and also drank some water that I discovered there. Then I lit my cigarette and was just about to look for some coffee when the Phoenix, who apparently could read my thoughts, said, "There is tea, coffee, everything you might need in the cupboards, including a stove; so please make yourself some coffee if you wish."

Astonished, I did so, and as we flew upward with extraordinary speed, I sipped my coffee.

In a short while the Phoenix spoke again: "In the last cupboard there is a large bottle. Drink a cup of what is in it. From the small bottle next to it take some kohl[3] and rub it around your eyes. Very soon we will be leaving the earth's atmosphere."

2. Phoenix: anqa or simurgh; a huge, extremely long-lived mysterious bird whom God originally created with all perfections.

3. kohl: an allusion to the Prophet Solomon's stibium by which he saw all secret things; collyrium which enables one to see the hidden treasures of the earth.

I quickly did as she ordered. As we flew, the blue of the sky deepened until it became absolutely dark. I found myself within a night more intensely dark than any I had ever experienced, but by means of the kohl around my eyes, I could see the millions of stars in the blue vault, the Phoenix, the articles on her back, and myself. After a while I looked back towards the earth and was startled to discern a narrow graveled road. It appeared quite close within my field of sight but stretched endlessly upwards. Encountering such a path in space surprised me so much that I expressed my astonishment to the Phoenix. She laughed and raised her beautiful claw to catch a large pebble. As she gave it to me, she said, "You now have the ability to understand the language of meaning spoken from heart to heart; speak with the stone."

I lit a cigarette and held the stone in front of me.

"O stone, what are you?" I inquired. "Where do you come from? Where are you going?"

As I listened, I began to hear a sad moaning in response.

"O human, again you've opened the floodgates of grief! What am I? I don't know. But when once I knew, I was a part of one of the countless dwellings in the universe. Though now I am small, twenty or thirty of the bits which compose me used to be part of the organs of famous scholars. I was also once within the organs of heroic kings. Like my peers I lived in those places removed from grief and sorrow, but one day a tremendous sound shook us, a terrific wind blew, and the home we had known exploded into billions of pieces. For millions of years my companions and I were forced to wander around a source of light and heat. At times I was bright, and at times I was dim, and in this way, time passed. A day finally came, I don't know why, when we found ourselves moving away from that light source. It was as if we had arrived at a place of neutrality between two universes. But again, the whip of the hand that drove us commanded, 'Move!' We became slaves of a different sun; we became its reflectors. And now, after so many millions of years, a new difficulty has arisen with which my friends and I have become preoccupied. While whirling around our new sun, we came upon a cloud of smoke. Some fell into this smoke, and as they burned, we heard them moaning, 'Ah!' The rest of us anticipated being burned at any moment. But the sad thing is: we don't know whether we will become nothing, whether we will be comfortable after we are burnt, or whether we will wander around again in another endless universe within still another entity. We just don't know."

The stone had finished its story, so I cast it back out into space. Once again perceiving my thoughts, the Phoenix informed me: "Yes, this stone is a remnant of a disintegrated universe. It served in the composition of a few comets, and it is in special service now around the sun. If it enters the atmosphere of the earth, it will become a shooting star like the others."

I fell into the depths of thought and, growing tired, fell asleep. When I awoke, I could feel moist air penetrating my lungs and discovered that we had come to rest upon a high hill. The view around us was overwhelming: an infinite ocean had covered the whole universe, and like pots of flowers, lush islands rose out of this sea, creating a panorama of extreme beauty. I could see that among the lovely grasses and strangely shaped flowers and trees that covered the islands there were strong, well-constructed houses built of porphyry. The Phoenix again guessed my thoughts and responded, "We are on another planet."

Overcome with wonder, I exclaimed, "How it resembles our world!"

"Yes," the Phoenix replied. "It is very similar but more perfect as it has had more time to evolve."

Again I inquired, "But aren't there any large continents here as there are on earth? Has a huge ocean overspread the whole planet? I see only thousands of small islands."

"It is the rainy season here now, so flooding has covered all but the mountainous areas which you thought were islands. When the waters recede, the land and seas will regain their usual boundaries. Because the overflowing of the rivers occurs regularly, the living creatures here have settled only on the heights. Long ago an intelligent creature who appeared here, the human of this planet, began a struggle against the harmful, wild animals. The cycling of the land into islands was helpful, so that at last he won the battle. Only the few useful animals survived, and as he nurtured them, they multiplied, and their species became perfected. No cities, or governments, or other such organizations exist on this planet. The perception of the people here is very unusual. They have no need of many of the things which you need. Take the telescope and watch them for a while; we'll set out again fairly soon."

I directed the telescope towards one of the houses and was startled to see creatures quite similar to earthly human beings. The only difference seemed to be that these people had more organs than we do. Once again I mentioned my surprise to the Phoenix.

"Why be astonished at this?" she inquired. "The form of the human being is the most beautiful of creation. Don't you see that everything is evolving towards the same form? The geometry discovered by man's perception exactly correlates to the art of nature. Well, it is this correlation which manifests the greatest evidence that man is the essence of the universe and that he has both a physical and a spiritual bond with the Creator."

We set off into the infinite field again and encountered thousands of small planets and many comets as we traveled over part of the heavenly path that had been formed from innumerable dissolved universes. One day we arrived near a very hot planet of strange plants and huge mountains, so high as to make the Himalayas seem like little hills.

The Phoenix spoke, "This is Jupiter."

The animals I could see here were roughly similar to our fossils of the cretaceous layer. We didn't linger but continued on until we at last came to the end of this solar system. In a balance that is almost imperceptible to us, the attraction and repulsion of the sun ultimately leads to dissolution.

We witnessed many other solar systems with one or two suns, containing thousands of inhabited worlds. The life forms and their organization were all similar; the source was the same. I was growing tired of it all and spoke with the Phoenix: "It's been almost a year since we set out on this journey. If we continued, could we ever reach the end of these solar systems?"

The Phoenix laughed. "We haven't yet watched even a millionth part of one of the thousands of universes already discovered by your scholars. Even if we were to fly quickly for millions of years, we would still be able to visit only a small fraction of this universe."

"O Lord! What is this? What is this bewildering sight?" I exclaimed.

"This is the great Kaf Mountain, the infinite mountain which covers the entire earth."

I fell silent.

At last she said to me, "Drink a little from the bottle in the third cupboard and gather your courage. Don't be afraid. You'll soon witness a sight no man has ever seen. Do you see the sun in front of the sun that is expanding? This sun is thousands of times larger than your sun. Watch! We'll go quite close."

As she increased her speed, I took the bottle out of the cupboard and drank some of the water. Still trembling with fear, I watched as this sun grew larger and larger. At first it seemed like a huge field, but then it expanded to fill the whole horizon until I beheld a sea of raging fire, whose waves were like mountains. Though we were still rather far away, we traveled through an atmosphere of light. As we came closer to the surface, the immensity of the burning waves increased until it was beyond the strength of a human being to bear it.

The Phoenix spoke: "You can't imagine the intensity of the terrible sound made by the boiling heat at the center of this sun. If we magnified the thunder of your world a million times, you might just begin to have an inkling of it."

Waves rising hundreds of kilometers high swelled one after the other. Such a hell was before me that I really could bear it no longer. I was just about to ask the Phoenix to turn around when that heavenly hell shook and the waves of fire at the surface crashed into each other with such force that they rose into gigantic mountains of fire whose peaks passed beyond sight. The surface of the sun cracked and split. Spewing out from this opening which was as large as the earth, more waves of fire, thousands of kilometers high, issued forth. Powerless before this terrible sight, I cried aloud with horror and fear. And then I fainted. . . .

When I opened my eyes I saw that I had fallen down from the grave of the turbaned one and now found myself lying on the bare ground. The Mirror Dede was brewing coffee. I went over to him. With a serious face, he spoke: "When the yeast is the same, a flea and an elephant are one. This is why the wise never fly all around the universe like the Phoenix. This ney is an empty thing. This grandeur, this endless sea that tears hearts apart cannot fill even a fraction of a small speck of Allah. Drink your coffee."

I kissed the honored hands of the Mirror Dede with a seriousness and sincerity rarely found within me, or any human being.

**

O Oneness! You are the endless, rolling sea!

Again it is You who is seen among the many waves. Though You have given Yourself a thousand names, a hundred thousand forms, whatever is said—the sky, the stars, the spirit of the body—is You, only You!

Even if the eye of man looks with intense attention at the universe—the sky, the blue vault, the sun, the world above, or this earth and this lowly soil—even if he looks at the face of Adam with the telescope of knowledge, it is You, only You!

In hyacinth and basil or in thistle; in the heart-rending roar of the lion or the sweet voice of the nightingale; in the bud that lends joy or the fragrance of the rose which uplifts the spirit; in the most lifeless particle; in the least of the animals—it is You, only You!

In all my senses; in heart, intellect, and conscience; when I am drunk and bewildered with the desire of love; and in the pain of the moments when I am separated from my beloved; in my uncertain soul that burns with longing—it is You, only You!

In my embrace, when the moon-faced beauty trembles; when in a moment infinity unfolds; when enraptured, I behold the snowy sky; in fear of grandeur when my soul is bewildered—it is never anything but You, only You!

CHAPTER SEVEN

The Sixth Day:
Kaf Mountain and the Phoenix

The Beneficent One, Who is Established on the Throne.
Qur'an XX:5

I was eighteen now and the son of the sovereign of India. One day a tremendous noise rose from the city beyond the palace walls. Everyone was rushing about, and even the people of the palace were greatly excited. I asked my tutor, a famous scholar and man of wisdom, what the reason was for all this bustling agitation.

He told me the following: "My prince, for a long time a dragon has been disturbing the borders of India. This fire-breathing dragon has seven heads and seventy legs, and its skin is so toughly armored that no sharp weapon can penetrate it. It can speak any language. Every seven years this terrible creature comes to us and demands, 'Where is this caravan leading?' No one understands the question. Which caravan? No one knows. Seven times the dragon repeats this question. When it still receives no answer, seven young men and seven virgins, all at the age of twenty, must be sacrificed to it. Then it calls out, 'I will return in seven years. You can learn the answer to my question from the Phoenix of Kaf Mountain.' Only then does it leave. Well, the time has come; the next seven years have ended and the dragon is expected to return today. By drawing lots we must choose seven young men and women and with heavy hearts surrender them to the dragon."

His story took me by surprise; I wanted to know more. "Where is this Kaf Mountain? Who is the Phoenix?" I asked.

My tutor answered: "There are many tales about Kaf Mountain, but we have never met anyone who has seen it or knows the truth of it. Some say that Kaf Mountain is an emerald mountain surrounding our world. According to others it is a single mountain at the center of the earth which rises beyond sight into the sky. But from where does one reach it? In which region of the earth is it located? There are those who immediately deny its existence, saying it is impossible that such a mountain could exist on this earth. As for the Phoenix, it is said to be a bird which has its home on Kaf Mountain, that it can speak, and that it lives for millions of years. Some people even claim it is immortal and is a scholar and a judge and aware of secret things. But again, there is no one who knows for sure; no one who has seen it."

That day the dragon appeared. It asked the seven customary questions and, when they went unanswered, took its sacrifices and left, plunging the city into mourning.

I was deeply affected by these events and could no longer sleep at night as I was thinking continuously about Kaf Mountain and the Phoenix. At last I made a decision. I went to my father and told him that I must go in search of Kaf Mountain in order to save our country from the dragon. I must find the Phoenix so that I might learn the answer to the dragon's question. My father was a very just and wise ruler. Though he knew I would probably die trying to accomplish my aim, he did not try to stop me. To take on a difficult task and to be willing to sacrifice one's life for it is a goal that suits sovereigns and their offspring. My father spoke, "Alright, my son! Make your preparations and let me also think about what will be necessary."

When the people were informed of my intention and determination, they came to kiss the threshold of the palace in gratitude and prayed throughout the night for my success. The next day my father gathered all the scholars and wise people, told them of my intention and asked them which way I should go. Many opinions were expressed, but after long discussions, a wizened, old doctor spoke: "My sovereign! This kind of journey is not possible with an entourage. With some precious jewelry in their belts one or two people can manage to live for years and can beg when necessary; for a crowd it would not be possible to eat and drink so easily or travel around freely in foreign countries. So it would be best for our prince to set out on this journey with only one companion. No one seems to know which direction he should travel. I cannot answer this either, but there is a solution. Beyond the Himalayas there is a place of seclusion. A wise man lives there who knows many things we don't know. Let the prince first go to him, become his servant, win his love, and then ask him about this unknown place he seeks. Let us hope that in this way he will succeed."

This suggestion was accepted by everyone. Finally one day, after receiving the good luck wishes and blessings of my father, the viziers, ministers, and scholars—after seeing the tears and hearing the parting prayers of hundreds of thousands—I set out towards the north of India. Bahadir,[1] the son of my tutor, accompanied me. Though many precious jewels were tucked into my belt, our load was light, and we were dressed in simple clothing. While we adjusted to the difficulties of the journey, we passed beyond the tops of the snow-covered peaks of the Himalayas. After many days of walking we at last found the retreat of the wise man we were seeking. I greeted him and told him of my goal and our situation. He raised his hand to his white beard and thought for a moment. At last he spoke:

"My son! I know many things, but I do not know the location of Kaf Mountain. However, seven months journey from here are the ruins of Milset. There is a well there whose opening is sealed with a very precious stone. Sometimes, for an unknown reason, this seal opens. You must go now and wait by the well. If you are fortunate and the stone moves, descend into the well with a rope. You will come upon a hole; go through it, and you will come to an open field. At the center of the field is a palace. Enter the palace but do not pay attention to

1. Bahadir: royal hero

anything that you see. Do not stop to rest and do not be afraid. Upstairs in a marble cupboard, you will find a box. Take it and return to the well. If you find the entrance to the well is still open, hold onto the rope and climb out. Then read the tablet that is in the box."

After readying the rope and preparing the other things that would be needed, I kissed the hand of this wise man, and we set out. Along the way we continually asked people the location of the ruins of Milset, until at last we arrived and settled down by the well to wait. At last, on the fortieth day after our arrival, the stone covering of the well began to move. Without losing a moment I quickly said good-bye to Bahadir, threw the rope down the well, and descended. As soon as my feet touched the ground, I untied the rope from my waist and looked around me for the hole. I soon saw it and, after hesitating for barely a minute, entered the opening and walked on. After a short while I came out into an open field. There was indeed a golden palace before me, surrounded by such a charming garden it brought me great joy just to behold it; but careful not to stop, I immediately entered the palace door. I paid no attention to any of the wonders I saw, nor ventured into any of the rooms I passed, but went straight upstairs to the room I was seeking. I found the cupboard and took the box out and, as quickly as I could, returned to the well. The stone had already begun to move back across the opening. Bahadir was shouting to me with all his might that the lid was closing. I immediately tied the rope to my waist and called to him to pull me up. I barely had time to climb out of the well before the stone had closed again. After heartily embracing each other, we turned to the box and with great difficulty managed at last to open it. Inside was a steel tablet upon which were written these verses:

Address to Me from My Secret

The rising place of the sun of essence and identity,
the origin of existence, is me.
I am the source of meaning, the dream of plurality,
the withinness of the body.
I am He that created the universe by my own command.
This existence is completely my creation.

I am endless time.
I am He who is beyond space, beyond time, and without limit.
I am the possibility that appears within every time, every space.
I am the throne of God, and the highest heaven
which sustains His throne, all His knowledge, and His power. I
am the seven heavens.
I am the substance, the essence, and the root;
the lifeless, and the living animal.
I am pure light, the absolute secret, the dot above the *nun*.[2]
I am both spirit and angel. I am man. I am Adam.
I am absolute essence,
apparent through my actions and attributes.
I am the Glorious Creator, the All-Compassionate One.

Answer from Me to My Secret

I am He, that when I say "I," I mean Your Omnipotence.
I am He that Your Oneness has appeared from me.
O body! If I assume that my oneness is separate from You,
I am in sheer delusion. Does nothingness ever have a body?
I am a fakir whose everything belongs to You. I am nothing.
The order of oneness, of voluntary poverty is at hand.
The highest heaven and the throne of God,
the earth and sky, all exist by Your word.
The pages of creation, Your holy verses,
have been written by Your grateful hand.
You are that essence who is beyond signs,
beyond space, beyond time!
All that exists belongs to Your attributes and action
and Your most supreme power.
Nothing exists but You.
Within every creature,
the secret of Your existence endures forever.

2. nun: an Arabic letter, ن , symbolizing the manifestation of creation; creation is the bowl manifested around essence, the single dot.

I was unable to understand the meaning of these words. On the other side of the tablet there was still no mention of Kaf Mountain. Overcome with sorrow I despaired of what to do next. Bahadir and I discussed our situation at length and finally decided to continue journeying towards the East and to ask about Kaf Mountain wherever we went.

For two years we wandered through various countries and passed through hundreds of cities. Nowhere could we obtain any information about Kaf Mountain.

One day we stopped in a large, attractively built city and were welcomed into a home as guests. After we had been there a few days, we heard criers walking through the streets announcing, "O people! Whoever brings the tablet preserved in the ruins of Milset and presents it to the head scholar may exchange it for a more important tablet upon which a great secret is written."

The tablet of Milset was with us! Even though we hadn't understood its meaning or usefulness, we had kept it. I immediately went to see the chief scholar and told him that I had the tablet he was looking for. He embraced me with great joy. He took the tablet of Milset and gave me the other one. I looked at this new tablet and saw that a poem was written on it also:

Every cycle in the universe
moves toward maturity and perfection.
Every dancing particle flies toward union
with the One Beloved.
Man and the world run
towards the dream that cannot be fulfilled.
If you are human, come and understand
what it is that's truly desired.
Don't give up; don't bring the holy wrath upon yourself.
Does the sun which rose in the infinite past,
ever cease to radiate?
Don't waste precious time.
Turn your face towards the perfection and beauty of God.

I was surprised by these words and told the scholar the reason for all our travels. He was surprised by our story and exclaimed: "A strange thing indeed! I took this tablet out of a well in the ruins of Nezara. I couldn't understand its meaning, so the wish which had inspired me to look for it remained unrealized. For years I continued to travel. At last, on the Serendip Island,[3] upon the Hill of Adam, I met a hermit. He told me, 'If you bring the tablet in the ruins of Milset to me, your wish will come true.' For years I looked for these ruins but was unable to find them. At last I returned sorrowfully to my own country, but made it a habit to send around criers every year calling for the tablet of Milset. And so at last, through you, I now have the tablet, but unfortunately the poem on this tablet doesn't help me either. Does it help you?"

"No," I replied.

We decided to go to Serendip Island together to find the hermit of the Hill of Adam and, bringing the two tablets with us, ask him for help. After a long journey we managed to arrive and found the hermit. We gave him the tablets and described our difficulties.

Astonished at us, he exclaimed, "Descriptions are useless without God's help." He turned to me, "O beggar! The poem on the first tablet tells about Kaf Mountain and the Phoenix." He bent over and whispered the necessary information in my ear. "The poem on the second tablet is the answer to the dragon's question. These creatures and universes, all of creation which is infinite in relation to us—these caravans, these systems, these suns and worlds—are within an endless space and extend beyond the highest heaven and throne of God. All are flying towards the unique secret, the light of Love which has no space, no sign. This dream show, this wheel of fortune cycles eternally."

The hermit also solved my friend's difficulty. With joy in our hearts we kissed his hands and set out once again for our own countries. Halfway home our paths parted, and Bahadir and I bid farewell

3. Serendip Island: the island where Adam landed following his fall; currently known as Sri Lanka, formerly Ceylon. "The Three Princes of Serendip," a Persian fairy tale in which the heroes make numerous fortuitous discoveries, was the source of inspiration for the common English usage of "serendipity."

to our scholar friend. Three months later we arrived in my father's kingdom. Seven years had passed since our departure. Our homecoming coincided with the time of the dragon's arrival. One more day and it would descend again upon the city. My father had become an old man, and the people were awaiting the coming of the dragon with great sorrow. As Bahadir and I had changed a great deal during the seven years, no one recognized us. I sent Bahadir to my father with a message, "A dervish has arrived who will answer the dragon's question. Have all the people gather outside the city in the morning, and let them prepare a celebration."

Overcome with joy and astonishment, my father was at first at a loss as to how to proceed. He gathered all the scholars and ministers, and after much consultation, they decided to do what I asked. With the rising of the sun, people could be seen leaving the city in large groups. I took Bahadir with me and went before the king who treated us with great respect. Because of the extreme importance of the situation, my father waivered between fear and the dawning of hope. It wasn't long before the dragon emerged and, surprised to see so many people gathered, shouted, "So you dare to do battle with me! With the fire of my breath I will burn you and all your country to ashes!"

An envoy was sent out to the dragon to tell it that a fight was not what was intended but that someone had appeared who would answer its questions.

The dragon demanded, "Bring this person to me!"

I walked forward and stood in front of the fiery one.

"O man! If you fail to answer my questions, I will not only devour you, but I will want seventy men and seventy women for your audacity, instead of the usual seven of each!"

My father was informed of this condition. He hesitated, but after my assurances of success, he finally gave me permission to proceed. The dragon asked the well-known question, "Where is this caravan going?"

The suspense was tremendous. It was as if the souls of everyone watching had come out from their bodies and had begun to fly towards the words that would come from my lips.

"O foolish dragon! These universes which are in need of evolution, this caravan that is the prisoner of fate, all of creation is running towards the secret of the unique dream, the light of Beauty, which is attracting everything that exists."

When the dragon heard these words, it gave a loud shriek and began to shake. Before our very eyes, the dragon became a young angel-faced girl of sixteen. We stood there astonished as the girl approached me and spoke:

"I am the most beautiful creature formed by God's powerful hand. This whole time, I have been a sixteen-year-old maiden, but fate had turned me into a dragon. My salvation depended upon the correct answers to my questions. You have succeeded in answering the questions and have freed me from the ugly form in which you saw me, and so have saved the lives of many people here. From now on I am your servant."

The joy of my people knew no bounds. Soldiers had to order them to become quiet so that my father might speak: "My beloved people! This young man of such virtue and perfection has saved you from a great disaster. Surely, no one could doubt that he might serve you further. I have become too old. The reason that I have continued to carry the burden of sovereignty has been the absence of someone qualified to replace my poor son who is lost to me. Now God has sent this virtuous young man to us. I wish to appoint him to take my place. May God bless his throne and his crown!"

He called me to him and embraced me. I could stand it no longer; holding his hands in mine, I cried, "Dear father! Can't you recognize me?"

With a cry of joy, my father fainted. As the people realized that I was indeed the prince, joy spread until everyone was happily embracing and congratulating each other.

I married the beautiful girl whom I had liberated, and at the same time, the seven young men and seven virgins who had been chosen by lot for the dragon were married to each other. My father retired to his place of seclusion. After appointing Bahadir as my vizir, I began to rule our kingdom.

One Friday, I went out riding. Somehow my horse stumbled and I was thrown to the ground. . . .

I opened my eyes.

CHAPTER EIGHT

The Seventh Day: The Sea of Grandeur and the Great Whirlpool

Science is but a dot.

Ali (May God be pleased with him)

*T*oday the Mirror Dede was quite joyful. He even attached another large mirror to his conical hat and added two big yellow tin pieces to his robe. His behavior didn't disturb me, for I felt the deep gratitude a disciple feels towards his teacher. I would have continued to respect him even if he had added rusty cans to his robe.

I asked the reason for his extraordinary joy.

He answered, "You know our barber, Haji Mullah;[1] his cat has given birth to a very lovely kitten that is as white as cotton."

I couldn't help being surprised. "Excuse me Dede, but I can't see the reason for such extreme joy over the birth of a kitten."

"It's all very simple. Cotton has given birth; both she and the kitten are healthy. So we'll perform a ceremony for her."

1. Haji Mullah: A haji is one who has been on religious pilgrimage to Mecca. A mullah is an Islamic religious leader.

"For the kitten?!" I couldn't avoid teasing. "Will there also be a ceremony when this honored offspring is named?"

"She has already been named." He laughed, "Isn't it strange that though people have been creating words for thousands of years, there still aren't enough words?"

Confused I asked, "What do you mean?"

"The mother's name is 'Cotton.' If we named her son 'Cotton' as well, it would be too redundant. But Haji Mullah wanted the kitten to have a name that would also express whiteness. We conferred for four hours. We thought about 'Snowy,' but found that too cold. 'Radiance' didn't stand up well to repetition. Haji Mullah wouldn't agree to plain 'White,' because he hates that word. (When he was a child learning geography, he was beaten for some reason about 'The White Sea'). So, I suggested 'Pink,' which is the name of Cotton's uncle, but Haji Mullah rejected it because, 'a white cat is not called Pink.' At last we named the kitten 'Harmless' and celebrated.

"You see, people have invented that which they call 'logic' in order to classify things and determine that everything they say appears 'logical.' If I tell you now that a son is born to a certain king and the people there are celebrating the event, you wouldn't be astonished. Probably you'd find that very normal, wouldn't you? But just think a moment. First of all, it is not known whether the child will live or not. Secondly, it is not known whether he will be a good man or not. Thirdly, since he is a human being, there is a strong possibility that he will incline towards corruption rather than hold to the good. Fourthly, as the son of a king, one would expect that he will be proud, tyrannical, egotistical, and most likely rather ignorant. Therefore, when no one blinks about the great festivities for such a child as that, why should the birth of 'Harmless' not be worthy of the joy of at least two people?"

Quite bewildered, I gazed at this strange man whose very sarcasms were a lesson in wisdom. He began to play the ney and sing:

O, heart! You are the light of the universe.
Every moment you determine the unknown.
You are the mirror of matter.
You are the seen, the admired.

The oneness and all existing,
    the well-known conscience,
the awareness and that which is signified,
    the high mountain, the existence of man,
You are the mirror of matter.
You are the seen, the admired.

The hidden manifests itself in phenomena.
The apparent determines the hidden.
You are the mirror of matter,
You are the seen, the admired.

Of tablets of existence, you are the oneness.
You are the oneness of the signs of God.
You are the mirror of matter.
You are the seen, the admired. . . .

I had fallen asleep but was awakened by the voice of town criers announcing: "A caravan is leaving for the city of Jabilsa.[2] Travelers may still join the caravan until evening. After that they will be left here."

In Tabari's[3] history, I had read of the existence of this strange city, but I had never been able to find it in any geography book, and I had concluded that it must be imaginary. Now a caravan was heading there. While my mind struggled with this puzzle, something else caught my attention: the ceiling and walls of the room in which I found myself were made of silver! I cried out and jumped up. As I did so, I caught sight of myself in a mirror. I screamed in horror, outrage, and sorrow, for I saw that I had but one eye in the middle of my forehead and only one arm, coming out of the center of my chest, and only one leg supporting me. I could walk, but I soon realized I was better at jumping. I could remember another way of walking, so this new, extremely limited way of moving felt loathsome and ugly to me. The fact that I had only one eye and one arm also alarmed me.

2. Jabilsa: the westernmost city with a thousand gates. In Sufism or *Tassawuf* it is the last destination, the final goal of the efforts of a human being.
3. Tabari: a famous Islamic historian.

"O Lord! What is this situation in which I find myself?" I was thinking when the door opened, and a woman came hopping into the room.

"The caravan is about to depart. All your things are ready. Let us say farewell."

I left the silver house only to discover that the whole city was made of silver. I managed to mount a donkey that had but two legs and caught up with the caravan just outside the city. Everyone else was formed in the same way that I was. I turned to a friend who happened to be next to me and asked, "How many days will it take to reach the city of Jabilsa?"

"Seven years," he replied.

To ride for seven years on a donkey that had only two legs seemed to me to be beyond anyone's endurance. I asked my friend, "What is this city called?"

He answered, "The city of Jabilka."[4]

Amazing! Here I was already in one of the two cities about which I had read in the history of Tabari but had never been able to locate. The odd thing was that I was a resident of this one and for some reason was on my way to the other.

I spoke to my friend again, "Why are we going to the city of Jabilsa?"

"Haven't we submitted a petition to the chief judge to be allowed to go there?"

"I can't remember why we submitted the petition," I confessed to him.

"That's strange. The reason for our petition is that we wish to have two arms and two legs."

Hearing these words, a heart-felt cry escaped my lips, and from that moment, I was determined to endure any difficulty in order to reach Jabilsa.

---

4. Jabilka: the easternmost city with a thousand gates. This city represents the first phase of a human being's journey towards God, the acknowledgement of inclination and intention.

It took us exactly seven years. When we arrived, we discovered this city was made entirely of gold. All the inhabitants came out to greet us calling: "What wonders God has willed! Here are the ones who were not content to remain with only one eye, who could not really walk with one leg, those who did not want to remain with only one arm! Welcome!"

Right away celebrations began and continued for forty days and forty nights. At last, under the command of an old, white-bearded man, we set out for the Heaven of Spiritual Knowledge. It was a mile beyond the city of Jabilsa, which is the end of the inhabited universe. It is impossible to fully describe the Heaven of Spiritual Knowledge, but I must tell you about one incredible aspect. Adjoining the beautiful garden of this heaven, to the western side, there was a sea. The edge of the sea was beside the garden, but its surface was not at the same level, and it stretched so infinitely high one could see no end to it. Even so, not a single drop from the sea spilled into the garden. It was as if there was a transparent Great Wall of China between the water of the sea and the air of the garden. The sight of this motionless sea, so quiet and endless, made my hair stand on end.

We remained in that heaven for quite some time, enjoying the pleasures of that place until one day we were led to a huge waterfall. What I will now describe may be beyond the ability of your intellect or imagination to accept, but a waterfall of wrath arose from the middle of the Sea of Grandeur and flowed towards the entrance of this heaven. This waterfall was called "Manifestation." The water flowing from it fell into the shell of a nut and disappeared within it. Petrified we stood transfixed before this bewildering sight.

When I collected myself a little, I cried out, "O Lord, what is this? How can this endless sea be flowing into this nutshell and still never fill it?"

Our guide heard my words and answered me, "So you see the Sea of Grandeur is disappearing like a pearl of nothingness into the Great Whirlpool. The water of this endless sea has been flowing into the Great Whirlpool from before the beginning of time."

Under the influence of this man of secrets we all watched in rapture. Then he spoke again: "For a moment you will hear the Waterfall of Manifestation, a sound which you have never heard before. The mere sound of it renders men powerless. But don't be afraid."

After a short while, at the very moment we began to perceive that intense vibration, we fainted, but it wasn't long before we regained consciousness. We soon realized that a major change had occurred: we now had two eyes, two hands, and two legs and feet. Everyone rejoiced and embraced . . . .

In the midst of this happiness I suddenly awoke to the Mirror Dede playing the ney and singing:

All this twoness is for oneness.
Look, two eyes see one!
And "one" is for peace.
Look, two eyes see one!

Spirit and body, the empyrean and heavens,
humanity and sprites, jinns and angels,
all this work is for oneness.
Look, two eyes see one!

Be awake to its harm;
don't spend your time vainly.
Throw a glance at the universe.
Look, two eyes see one!

So do you; so also do you.
Know that this is "what my Lord has taught me."[5]
Make the soul and the flesh one and see.
Look, two eyes see one!

---

5. "what my Lord has taught me": This is the exact parallel to the moment referred to in Surah Yusuf (XII:37), when Joseph speaks of his duty to convey truth and faith.

CHAPTER NINE

The Eighth Day:
The Eternal Mystery

Those who are firmly rooted in knowledge . . .
Qur'an III:7

When I closed my eyes, I found myself among a few hundred students seated before a teacher of majestic presence. As I shifted my position, I put my hand on my head and was surprised to feel a twisted lock of hair at the top of my head. Then I remembered that I was Chinese. Suddenly, I remembered many other things as well.

I was a young man from the city of Nanking who had been receiving an education in science and spiritual knowledge. After having traveled extensively in my own country, I had continued my pursuit of knowledge and had arrived in India where I happened upon things I did not understand and could not explain. I had sought answers from the wisest men in India, but none of them had been able to provide me with an answer that would satisfy my heart. At last they had advised me to seek out a certain sage who had withdrawn from the world. He was said to be an exceptionally virtuous man among the Brahmans. I finally found him living in a temple in the middle of a forest filled with tigers, snakes, and poisonous plants, and I was now sitting in front of him for the first time. After a long silence, he addressed me with a voice that sounded as though it were coming from the grave, "O young man of China! What is the problem that you cannot solve? What are you looking for?"

"The eternal secret!" I replied.

The other students all looked at each other in amazement. It was clear from the way they regarded me that they were all seeking the same thing.

The Brahman began to speak again, "Which one?"

"Which one?"

"Yes, of course, which one?"

"The truth of the spirit," I answered.

The Brahman fell back into silence. His face became as pale as a dead man and his features more and more lifeless. After a while, he spoke, "The living cannot know spirit. Are you prepared to die?"

"Yes!"

"Come near me!"

I went close to him, and he spoke these words into my ear, "Imprison your animal spirit as much as you can, while continually chanting, 'my home, my home, my home.' Allow these men to take you to the place of seclusion."

They led me to a narrow, dark room large enough for only one person. I entered and began chanting, "My home, my home, my home." An inexplicable anxiety filled my heart. By evening I was becoming rather hungry; yet the door to this place of seclusion remained closed. Though I knocked on the door a few times in order to be let out, no one responded. At last, late that night, a servant came and let me outside for five minutes. He gave me a handful of roasted corn and a cup of water and said, "These make the animal impulses stronger, but you are not yet ready for asceticism, so for a few days these will be given to you."

I remained in this strange prison for seven years. After some time had passed, I was given the handful of corn every two days and then every three days. After five years I received a handful of corn only once a week, and that was sufficient. Water was then given to me once every fifteen or twenty days. At the end of the seventh year, I was taken out of my place of seclusion and brought before the Brahman into an area where hundreds of Brahmans and thousands of students had gathered.

My state had become impossible to describe. Gravity no longer had the same effect upon me; when I walked, I had a strange feeling of flying. If I didn't pay close attention, things around me became quite blurry, as if colors had lost their distinction. If I continued looking attentively at something for a while, surrounding things gradually disappeared. I no longer felt myself as matter but felt I consisted only of energy. Whomever I regarded, it was as if I could see or read the thought which troubled his heart.

When I went into the Brahman's presence, I approached him and kissed his hand. The sound created by this simple movement was surprisingly loud. Thousands of people began crying, "My home, my home, Brahma, Brahma." When I looked around I saw the reason for the outcries. The Brahman and I were standing together in the air midway between the floor and the ceiling. The Brahman held my hand, and walking in the air, we came up to the wall, but the wall did not stop us. Was it slit so that we were able to pass through, or did the wall lose its density? I don't know, but when we entered the room on the other side, the Brahman spoke, "I think we have solved the eternal secret now. You have known spirit."

"No," I answered, "I still don't know what spirit is."

"Great Brahma," he said. "Haven't you yet realized that you are spirit yourself?"

"I? Am I spirit?"

"Great Brahma! When you are flying through air and walking through walls, do you still doubt?"

"Doubt? I don't doubt; I am sure that I am not spirit. I am a corpse, and this corpse will disassociate tomorrow, and my ego will be nothing. I will no longer remain."

The Brahman uttered a loud cry. Several times, he exclaimed, "Great Brahma!" and then he fell down and died.

Immediately I threw myself over his corpse. Already his body was as cold as ice, and his heart had ceased beating. Yet in spite of this, he opened his eyes for a moment and spoke almost inaudibly, "Did you realize spirit?"

Just as I was answering, "No," laughter burst forth, tearing at my heart. I raised my head. Though the corpse still lay before me, the Brahman was now standing between the ceiling and the floor. He asked me, "Did you realize spirit?"

Before I had a chance to answer, the door opened. Someone entered and said, "They are calling you."

I followed the man into the room from which I had passed with the Brahman. To my great astonishment, I beheld the Brahman sitting there in his customary seat. He called me to him and began conversing again, "Have you still not realized spirit?"

"No, no! But if you would do me a favor and tell me about it?"

"Tell you about it! Tell you? Haven't we shown you?"

"Yes! But I did not understand. To see a thing is not enough to understand it."

"So!"

"One has to die," I said.

"Oh! Alas! To die, to die. This is what is impossible."

"Why?"

"Because, in order to die, first one has to be. This is the aim of my wisdom. Yet you are not content with this much. Now there is only one thing left to do. Do you have enough power to sacrifice your eternal life?"

"If I sacrifice my eternal life, what will I gain in understanding spirit?"

"Nothing! Since you will become nothing, naturally you cannot then gain anything."

"What is promised for us in eternal life?"

"Brahma gives good news of eternal pleasure for his friends."

"But in this eternity will this thought of wanting to realize what spirit is remain in me?"

"No doubt! You will remain with all your existence."

"Then I will sacrifice such a dreadful eternity. O dear Lord! I do not want to live eternally with this anxiety which gives me no peace. I don't want to; I cannot."

"Then come with me."

The Brahman held my hand again and took me to another room.

He took a piece of paper out of a vault. The names of seven people were written on it. "In seven thousand years, only seven people have come who have sacrificed their eternal lives in order to learn the spiritual sciences. You are the eighth. Write your name here."

I wrote my name on the paper. Again the Brahman spoke, "Go to the Mountain of Light. There your problem will be solved."

Leaving the temple behind, I set out towards the Mountain of Light. Sometimes I walked on the ground; sometimes I flew in the air. As I was passing through the valley in front of the mountain, I saw a baby who had just stepped into the world of nothingness. He lay in the middle of the way. Wondering who had left this poor baby there, hoping to see his mother or a relative, I looked around as I approached him. When I had come near him, the child spoke, "O seeker of knowledge! O man of anxious heart! Welcome!"

Bewildered to hear a newborn baby speak, I exclaimed, "At this age, when you are not even a year old, you are speaking! What a strange child you are!"

"Not only do I speak, I am rather talkative. Though you didn't ask, let me tell you my name. I am called 'Gnosis,'[1] the third step in spiritual knowledge."

"I was hoping to solve the eternal secret."

"And for this you sacrificed your eternal life in order to be free from the anxiety of the spirit!"

"Yes, this anxiety. . . ."

"O you poor, crazy man! This anxiety is the eternal anxiety of the whole universe, all of existence. No individual, no particle can be saved from this anxiety because they cannot fulfill the necessary conditions."

"What are these conditions? I sacrificed my life for this knowledge. Surely there cannot be a more difficult condition than that."

---

1. gnosis: *marifat*, divine wisdom; the skill or state of being wise, when miracles are manifested; the state of *arif*-hood (*arif*: the knower). This is the third of the four stages of progress from outer to inner. The other stages are: *shariat*, the religious law; *tariqat*, the mystical path and brotherhood; *marifat*, divine wisdom; *haqiqat*, Truth, where we meet and know the reality of God—not by means of the intellect or senses but by means of loving mind (*gonul*) and the whole of our existence.

"Is that what you think? In my opinion, if this condition were enough to realize what spirit is, there would be lots of people who would have done it. But, the special condition. . . ."

"What is this special condition?"

"To prove that nothingness and existence are the same—one single thing."

Hearing this impossible condition I sighed deeply. . . .

Opening my eyes, I saw the smiling, loving face of the Mirror. "Who can prove that nothingness and existence are the same, a single thing? Even this statement is crazy. Who could prove it?" I asked.

"Who?" The Mirror Dede replied, "The mad one who accepts knowing and not knowing as equal!"

CHAPTER TEN

The Ninth Day:
The Highest Court

Whatever their ways are, they are all in love with You.
Each comes, by a path, to the rose garden.
Niyazi Misri

*T*oday the Mirror wasn't shining as usual; sadness covered his face. We sat in silence for a long while, meditating. I thought over all the strange things that I had observed during my time with him and was amazed at the variety of contradictory ideas mankind has formulated. The words of the Mirror stirred me from my thoughts: "I don't wish to play just the ney for you, but the saz[1] as well."

He entered his hut, brought out a saz and, after some improvisation, began to sing:

> O pious ones, don't criticize us
>   with offensive, wounding words.
> Our hearts know the True Name.
> Don't talk to us of myths.

1. saz: a long-necked stringed folk instrument often used to accompany mystical songs.

Our way takes us to the Divine.
The ways of the saintly are many;
we say "yes" to all of them.
Call us "mad," we don't mind.
To be mad is better than to be well-behaved.
May God, the Life-giving, help you to live.
Glory be to life. If you are a lover, praise be to life.
Our clothing is evidence of our state. . . .

I had fallen asleep and now saw that I was in front of a tiny window inside a huge palace. Through this window I could see a room that was large enough to hold thousands of people. On all sides of the room were small windows like the one through which I gazed. A man sat at each window, watching the room beyond. Seated at ornate lecterns of emerald and ruby were proud, majestic beings with crowns on their heads. Most of their faces were veiled. Some of the seats were placed at a higher level than the others and were more richly decorated. The highest seat in the middle was empty. One of these majestic beings rose and began to speak,

"Humanity has arrived. He wishes to ask a question of us. Will you agree to hear him?"

Those who were present voiced their assent, and Humanity was ushered into the room. This person called "Humanity" appeared poor, crippled, and miserable. His old, wornout clothes and sallow complexion contrasted strangely with the magnificence of the others gathered there. The representative for the chief of the assembly spoke, "O Humanity! Sit down, relax, and ask your question."

Humanity continued to stand. "Sit down and relax? For hundreds of thousands of years, have I ever found time to sit and relax? The difficulty of earning a living and all the thousands of illnesses that beset my body, do they ever leave me time to rest? I am miserable, but still I cannot commit suicide. Yet I am worthless—worthless and miserable!"

Humanity wept, his breath catching spasmodically. Silence descended upon the assembly as they sat, deeply affected by Humanity's words of despair. Again the representative spoke, "Your problem is a difficult one; the solution depends upon the arrival of the head of our assembly."

Humanity pleaded, "At least if I could only see why I endure so much poverty, why I don't commit suicide. . . ."

Another member of the assembly stood: "If I may, let me attempt to console him a little." The rest nodded their assent, and he began to recite:

O Lord! What is this taste of life,
this strange power that binds one to living?
Life is fleeting, filled with trouble and grief.
Yet it is the goal; what is its hidden meaning?
Not for a moment is man left in comfort:
  always a thousand kinds of lament;
  making one's way is never easy.
When an infant, he cries in the cradle;
the time of innocence passes with screams of longing and pain.
When he is young, a thousand ambitions propel him;
When he is old, a thousand afflictions torment him.
At death the past is but a single moment.
Is all this misery for just one moment?
A secret voice intimates the answer:
for the wise, the pleasure and value of life is in beauty.
For the ignorant it is merely gluttony and lust.

Humanity sighed, "It's true! Tell me; have pity on me! Since I hate life and gain no pleasure from it, what good is happiness? Tell me, please."

Just then the leader of the assembly came in. He immediately saw the problem and, addressing the assembled majestic beings, said, "Yes, please; help solve the problem of this poor man."

Abraham, the friend of God, spoke first, "Happiness consists in working to earn one's livelihood and sharing what one earns with one's own kind."

Moses added, "Happiness is to save yourself from the tempting ambitions of Pharoah."

78

Adam spoke next, "Happiness is in not obeying Satan—the pride of one's own ego—or the whispers of Eve."

Confucius offered, "Simply to find all tastes in a pot of rice is Happiness."

Plato said, "Happiness ensues when one continually thinks about the highest, most majestic ideas."

Aristotle put forth, "Logic! That is Happiness!"

Zarathustra reflected, "Happiness is not to remain in the dark."

Brahma contributed, "Happiness? The opposite of everyone's opinion."

Jesus[2] spoke, "Happiness is possible if one forgets the past and accepts the present, while not worrying about the future."

Luqman[3] said, "People have invented this word to express all their sorrow with a single word."

Khidr[4] said, "Happiness is a phantom that sometimes sparkles like lightning in hearts free of ambition."

After all these words, Buddha stood up. "O Humanity! Happiness is one of the names of beauty and emptiness. Nirvana! O Humanity! Nirvana!"

Humanity slumped to the floor murmuring almost inaudibly in despair, "O, which of these is the truth? Which one?"

The leader of the assembly rose and spoke gently. "Humanity, happiness is to accept life as it is, and to surrender oneself to hard work, attempting to better oneself."

Humanity raised himself and replied, "O Glory of the Universe! You are the only one who understands humanity's trouble, and you have found the remedy. . . ."

2. Jesus: This quote probably refers to the parable of the lilies of the field. The availability of texts of world religions was rather limited during Ottoman times when Hilmi wrote *Awakened Dreams*. The "remedies" presented here are obviously encapsulated versions of much more complex philosophies.

3. Luqman: Often referred to as Luqman the Wise, he is considered by many to be one of the prophets. Some say he was the teacher of Pythagoras. Referred to in the Qur'an in Surah Luqman (Surah XXI).

4. Khidr: The mysterious prophet who drank of the water of eternal life, the elixir of immortality. He often appears suddenly when one is in extreme need. Khidr corresponds to Elijah.

When I opened my eyes, I looked for the Mirror, but could not find him. Instead, my eyes caught sight of a piece of paper lying near me. Upon it were written these words: "Farewell! A day will come when we will meet again."

I wept in sorrow until nightfall.

The Second Book

CHAPTER ELEVEN

The Lunatic Asylum of Manisa

(Some years later . . .)

A letter to Raji from his friend Sami:

Dear Raji,

I thought you would be sick for a while after that drinking spell.
I guessed right it seems, though I had pictured you coming down with
tuberculosis or anemia. Instead, I've heard you caught an illness for
which I can find no better term than "insanity."

Dear friend, what is going on? When I think that you were my
teacher in the way of Truth, it drives me crazy. I will always remember the old days and the extraordinarily eloquent talks we shared sitting beside the sea, but now I am confused. Is this Raji that clever master?
Or is he but one of thousands of fools? What are you seeking? What
do you want? Unless you are willing to refute established truths with
the truths that you've recently discovered, there is nothing we can do
but assume you have lost your mind.

What are you searching for? Eternal life? Poor fellow! What have
you found in this temporary life that would make you want to seek
its eternal counterpart?"

Taine[1] hits the nail on the head. He says, "From the viewpoint of creation and education, men are insane. Even if accidentally they are wise from time to time, it is exceedingly rare."

How true. If man really had a tiny bit of intelligence or wisdom, instead of looking for eternal life, he would—without ever enduring this wretched, temporary existence—present his head to the Sultan of nothingness and give it up! But I guess I have to admit that though this life consists only of misfortune and accident, there is still enough pleasure in it to entertain a lunatic.

Throughout the various ages of bestiality and confusion, people have invented words to convey spiritual ideas. Embellished with the colors of fantasy, these words have evolved through thousands of centuries. We have inherited them and now attribute thousands of kinds of heart-deceiving colors to this chain of words—words which are existentially "a nothing," and whose information is imaginary. This mass of matter has no value, no reality, nor essence. We are sweetly deceiving ourselves. We find "meaning" in life. Well, here is real life in all its ugliness!

Poor fellow! What are you looking for? As if this obscurity, this material existence, these visible illusions are not enough to crush one's spirit and put one's conscience in turmoil, do you want to run after spiritual phantoms too?

My poor brother, my poor master! I don't know whether you are in a state to even be able to read this letter or whether you will be able to realize the sorrowful moaning and pity pouring from my heart. They told me . . . but I don't want to believe that. I could not believe it. I couldn't stop myself from writing this letter to you. Answer me! For the sake of the old days, for the sake of the sweet memories, answer me!

Sami[2]

1. Taine: Hippolyte Adolphe Taine (1828-1893), a French historian and philosopher.

2. Sami: The All-Hearing One. One of the ninety-nine names of God in the Islamic tradition. He who hears sounds which can be heard, as well as those which are inaudible; he who hears the unspoken words of the heart.

***

Raji's reply:

Dear Sami,

I received your letter. Leaving the depths of dreams for five or ten minutes, I came out into this world, this dark hole. My boy! Since you believe that the world is a lunatic asylum and that people are mad, why does my madness bother you? Perhaps I have a passion for a different kind of madness.

Yes, my dear friend, I am looking for the ghosts that are hidden behind these illusions. What a pity. I can't find them. Actually it's not that I can't "find"; I don't know how to explain. . . .

There is not much to be said about scientific truths. But the existence of this kind of truth cannot stand in the way of another kind of truth. Some hearts are not satisfied by truths that try to divide the beginning from the end. I am determined not to leave this world without really understanding this life—why we came here, what we are to be, and who sent us. Alas! If only I could either resolve or dismiss these questions!

These questions which pain my heart don't have simple answers; they cannot. Those who listen only to the body, have an insensitive heart, and also ignore the discoveries science has made, can reject the ultimate truth. But to accept it without knowing or really seeing it is no better. I looked for a solution to my difficulty within the world of science but could find none there. Then I fell into a strange world. Perhaps those I found in this world would be able to convince many another conscience, but not mine. My heart's eyes can see the distant universes which telescopes cannot find. I am able to be in contact with enlightening stars whose essence our comrades have not yet even discovered. My eyes can see the darkened celestial bodies which hide from man's investigations—because I do not need light. I have become such a spirit that qualities like distant or near, dense or subtle, have no significance for me. Materiality is the prisoner of my command, and spirituality is helpless before my will. But still I am hungry! My spirit has not yet found the food of contentment that would satisfy it. I am still searching, searching. Will you ask, "What for?" Nothing!

Dear, beloved Sami, why do you see one more lunatic in this asylum as one too many? I can see that you feel sorry for me. Thank you, but I am like those opium eaters who, though they may appear weak or exhausted, enjoy their drunkenness. My greatest pleasure is the inquiry of my anxious conscience. Yesterday, I was wandering around the cemetery where we "troubled ones" observe life. I saw a mad man there playing with a balance scale. I asked him what he was doing.

"I am weighing foolishness and knowledge," he told me.

"What is your aim in doing this?" I inquired.

"To see whether there is something or not."

"O! Let me see what you've found!"

"My foolishness is so heavy that I think I am the Croesus[3] of the time!"

What does this mean? It's difficult to explain to you, but this is my situation. If there were something I needed in the world, I would seek your help, but I need nothing. I have but one request: forget me, in order that words may not take up my time.

Raji

***

One month after the arrival of this letter, Sami went to Manisa. His aim was to meet with his former master and honored friend, Raji, and to save him from such an unsavory life. He found Raji in the cemetery of Ayn-i Ali Sultan. Contrary to what he had expected, Raji was in good health. Yet, his clothing resembled that of the most hopeless beggar. When Sami entered the cemetery, he found Raji among the wild mallows, leaning against a grave. A woman who had entered the

---

3. Croesus: The last king of Lydia (c. 560-546 B.C.) who was known for his immense wealth.

cemetery just before him was also approaching Raji. Both of them reached him at the same time. Barely nodding, Raji acknowledged his visitors with astonishing indifference. In vain Sami tried to revitalize this statue with his kisses, and in vain he sought a spark of love in those extinguished eyes.

At last, Raji spoke, "Why did you come, Sami? To look at a gravestone?"

Bewildered, Sami's face filled with sadness. He could not believe that this was the same Raji whose manners had been imitated by the most refined, most eloquent young men.

"Woman! Why did you come?" Raji demanded.

As exuberant hearts do when they make an appeal, the poor woman emptied her tears like a flood as she answered: "O, my sheikh! O holy fool! O beloved God! My poor beautiful daughter! She went mad at the age of fifteen. I didn't even know what was happening. O! How could I know? All the while, my poor daughter was drowned in melancholy. She was in love, but my poor baby loved hopelessly, silently, in secret. She was in love with the son of Mr. Hutfullah. The poor young man fell off a horse. His head hit a stone and was crushed to pieces. As soon as my girl heard of it, she went mad! Wild with grief, she threw herself on the ground and began biting her own flesh. The neighbors tried to help me stop her, but it was helpless. Her cries were unendurable. We had to put her in an insane asylum. Now my beautiful one is in a lunatic asylum! I've sold everything I own. I've made vows at tombs, seeking the answer to my prayers. I've bought amulets and had prayers said for her. None of it was of any use. At last I was advised to come to you. They told me, 'Go and plead with him. Don't leave until he agrees to help your daughter. Surely, he will be able to help her.' For God's sake, O holy father, heal my daughter!"

The poor woman sobbed bitterly, but no sign of sorrow could be seen on Raji's face. Sami was astonished, for the pitiful state of this innocent mother had pierced his own heart, while her intense grief had not even affected Raji as much as the sound of a distant flute. He felt hatred boil up within himself towards Raji. Unable to contain himself, Sami burst out, "If I didn't know that you are unbalanced and so are not to blame, I would accuse you of cruel insensitivity!"

Raji stood up and spoke like a true lunatic: "Me? Am I the one who is unbalanced, deprived of common sense? Idiot! While you remain crushed by this catastrophe of life, I was thinking about what love is—how a person could possibly love himself when there is no twoness. I was thinking that when I and you and the air, the stone, the iron are all one thing, why does the iron not cry, the stone not go mad, but man. . . ." He broke off with a strange laugh. "You see, if a man speaks with the mad like you, he can't know what to think. I said that the iron doesn't cry. Who says so? What is the difference between iron and this woman? So who is it that weeps and that doesn't weep?" Holding and twisting Sami's arm, he continued, "Look, I have twisted this arm of yours. If there were only nothing besides you, who would twist your arm? But it is twisted. Why? There is no answer to this 'why'!

"Why is there love? Why is there poverty? Why is there pleasure? Why is there intense sorrow? Why? Why? There is no answer, is there? A fifteen-year-old girl and a young man at the age of twenty. . . alright, let the young man marry this girl, and let them be happy. But, no. The boy falls off the horse, and the girl goes mad. Why? Again there is no answer. Now why does this old woman live? And what pleasure is there in my life? Nothing. When everything is so, the boy dies, and the girl goes mad; the old woman and I live. Isn't it strange? There is nobody who knows why this is so, nobody, nobody!

"You feel pity for this old woman; yet you don't feel pity for me. Her daughter has gone mad, all right, but my spirit, my universe, went mad. Still, man's eye sees only the lowest of both pleasures and torments. Oh! Why did you find me? I was about to annihilate the difference of contradiction in this world. Why did you bring me back? Why did you make me descend again into a world with 'whys'? Oh! A body without 'why'! So, what difference is there between you and your daughter, this stone, and me? The body without I!"

***

Raji's excited state developed into what appeared to be extreme madness, and he was taken to the Manisa lunatic asylum. Within a few days his anger had subsided, and he was released into a courtyard of the asylum where the less violent lunatics spent their time. In the middle of this courtyard was a pool. Lunatics bathed openly in this pool and would wander about the courtyard naked. The Manisa asylum was then a place of terrible poverty: the beds on which the patients slept were filthy, and the food was exceptionally poor. Occasionally, people would come to watch the mad ones through the bars of the courtyard and would pass things to them. Some of the lunatics could not distinguish between good and bad and would often end up eating things that were inedible. Some of the mad were given boring, useless jobs to keep them busy, but the only therapy ever offered within the asylum was the pool. Whenever anyone became violent, they were hurled into it.

Fate had driven Raji to such a place. It was quite easy to enter this asylum; according to the entry-keepers, everyone who was brought to the asylum was mad. But because there was no measure of sanity, it was very difficult to get out of the asylum—especially if no one was particularly interested in your case and inquiring about you.

Raji was a stranger to this part of the country. His breakdown had passed, but to someone in his state, the most joyful and comfortable place to be is an insane asylum. The strange opinions of the lunatics kept him from thinking. He decided to stay at the asylum for a while and so made no attempt to leave.

To investigate madness is possibly one of the most sensible things to be done by those who claim sanity. Here are some of Raji's observations from the Manisa asylum:

The Lunatics of Ambition

At the Manisa asylum, among my friends who had gone mad were many who deserved close scrutiny, who made me deeply consider whether madness is a catastrophe or might be a blessing. Within the universe everything is relative. Under these conditions madness is sometimes a disaster but sometimes a happy occurrence.

Among the harmless mad ones there was a soldier of the gendarmes who thought he had become the regiment commander. Everyday he used to sit for hours in a corner, deep in thought. Finally he would stand up with a big smile on his face. One day I went over to him and asked him what he was thinking about. He replied:

"There are about a thousand bands of brigands. The Black Brigand, the White Brigand, the Green Brigand, and the Purple Brigand have all gone up into the mountains. I am the regiment commander of all of Turkey, so the Grand Vizir has ordered me to catch these brigands. I've sent about a thousand troops. I've put my wisdom into a plate, divided it into a thousand pieces, and have put a part of it in the bag of each troop sergeant. When the sergeants cannot solve a problem, they take my wisdom out of their bags and ask for advice. So now, neither the Black Brigand nor the Purple brigand can threaten us any longer. I have caught them. The Sultan has at last been told of our success, and as a reward has given me forty female servants, a camel load of gold, and five hundred medals. Here was my problem: if I put these medals together with the medals I had already received, they would fill twenty rooms. How was I to carry them? At last I found a solution: I rented a train. Wherever I go I'll take my medals with me; they'll be hung in the wagons, and I'll have it written in large letters, 'These medals belong to the regiment commander, the Chirping Brigand.' There is nothing else to be done. If a man can't have his medals with him, what use are they?"

This poor one was among those who were happily mad. When I reflected on the fact that there were thousands of crazy people in this system, I had to ask myself whether perhaps the world is nothing but a huge lunatic asylum.

**

The Double Hafiz

Within the asylum there were two people who spent a great deal of time together. One of these two madmen was a hafiz, someone who knew the Qur'an by heart and could recite it. The other was a cartwright. They were referred to as "The Double Hafiz," because the cartwright was always imitating the hafiz.

Sane people often came to the courtyard bars to watch the mad. With the habit of generosity characteristic of all Muslims, they often gave out small gifts of tobacco, or sugar, or other treats. As soon as the greedy ones among us saw someone come to the bars, they would go over to them, start babbling according to their particular specialization, and ask for tobacco and other things.

The hafiz had been accustomed to reciting prayers at funerals, at the bedside of the sick, and at weddings, so when he saw someone approaching the bars he would go in front of them, kneel down, and begin to pray. The cartwright would then kneel down next to him and try to imitate the words and manner of the hafiz so that he might earn a share of whatever the hafiz earned. From time to time, the poor hafiz would caution those who watched, "Don't listen to him. He is not a real hafiz."

But the cartwright would wink and say, "Don't pay attention to his words; poor man, he's mad."

One day when I was talking with this false hafiz, I asked him how he could pretend to be a hafiz. He told me: "Ninety percent of the people who listen to a hafiz are incapable of discerning if his reading is correct. Whatever a man recites for them, they think that it's the Holy Qur'an and just swing their heads. Our hafiz himself doesn't understand what he is reciting. Is it any wonder that most of those who watch us swear that I am a hafiz?"

***

A Madman Whose Madness is More Sensible Than His Wisdom

There is a class of people among us who not only profess what they know, but also claim to be authorities in every other area as well. Though one is not trained as a doctor, he looks down on whatever doctors recommend and gives his own medical advice to anyone he meets. Though another doesn't really know much about marriage and has a wife who is ugly both in heart and body, yet he authoritatively teaches the ways of marriage to every young man. The house which another spent lavish amounts of money to build ends up looking like a stall; yet he expresses nothing but criticism for a master architect like Sinan who overcame great obstacles to create mosques of exquisite beauty.

One such man I knew at the asylum had owned vineyards. Because he had no idea how to make a living, he had lost most of his fortune. This was a shock to him, but still it didn't bring him to his senses. He had heard that phylloxera, a disease affecting his vines, was caused by tiny creatures and, finding the cautions of the agricultural inspector extremely ignorant, attempted to make his own insecticides. Having observed that mercury repels lice, sulphur ointment cures scabies, and antimony is useful for certain wounds, he prepared a paste of a mixture of these with other repellents and rubbed it on his vines. The result? The same result as Dr. Blankshot's cure for toothache: to cure toothache, this wise philosopher used to recommend the extraction of the jawbone.

**

Fifteen days after Raji had entered the asylum someone new arrived. The less mad ones welcomed him and gathered around to serve him. The older lunatics recognized him as one they had known and loved before. While this newcomer walked about the courtyard with dignified steps and a smiling face, twenty or thirty lunatics all began yelling, "The Mirror, the Mirror, the Mirror!"

Raji's attention was caught, and he raised his head. A cry of joy and astonishment escaped his lips: the new arrival at the asylum was the Mirror Dede whom he had lost. Though he had traveled over half of Anatolia in search of the Mirror Dede, he had found no trace of him. Now, as if helpless before a compelling magnetism, he reached out to grasp the hands of the Mirror.

CHAPTER TWELVE

The Deepening Of Dreams

The only real knowledge of man
is to admit that he knows nothing.

*S*ince our time together in the asylum, I hadn't seen the Mirror for quite a while. The first chance I had, I went to visit him again at his place of retreat in the cemetery next to the mosque. His first words were: "O, my son! Where were you? We have been waiting for you for such a long time."

"Yes, I had to accept the ways of the world for a while. Otherwise, separation from the blessing of your presence would have torn me apart."

After chatting a bit about unimportant things, he said, "May the blessings of the saints be with us! Let's drink some coffee," and he placed a pot on the burner.

We were drinking our sweet coffee when. . . .

Suddenly, I found myself in part of an ant colony whose nest had thousands of passages. I looked around in admiration. The ants had been divided into several different social classes, but the classes were unlike those among humans. There was no real difference of rank between what might have been called their "aristocracy" and "the general populace"; distinctions such as "high" or "low" didn't really exist. There were at least one or two hundred thousand ants in the nest, divided for practical purposes into a class of masters and a class of workers. They had developed a language with which they could express and satisfactorily respond to any kind of mental or physical need. Within this nest were perfect schools, granaries, jails, dormitories, dining rooms, and meeting halls—in short, all the complexity of a city. It was strange that the society of these ants was more highly evolved than that of mankind. For example, the cooperation among workers was of a much higher level and this resulted in a much better functioning economic system. The ants also far surpassed mankind in manners. Without hesitation I would say the same about their legal system. In addition, schools occupied the largest and most elaborate parts of the nest, while prison areas were quite small in comparison, for almost no one was sentenced to jail. It was obvious that an ant's first priority and its supreme virtue is a feeling of responsibility for its work. This focus predominates over every other feeling; no ant would ever sacrifice his work for the sake of bodily needs or passions. A lazy ant does not exist.

I happened to be the son of one of the master ants. After consulting with other masters, my father chose seven elders from the working class and seven famous scholars to supervise my education. These seven scholars were the most advanced in knowledge and virtue among not only the inhabitants of our nest but among those of surrounding nests as well. These elders—who had arrived at the last stages of their lives and were now prepared to surrender—tried hard to help me become a useful member of the ant community. They wished to bring one last student to maturity. As they were excellent teachers, in a very short time they had taught me almost all the sciences known to the ants. Now I traveled frequently with them as we busied ourselves applying the things which I had learned.

One morning when my servants realized that I was awake, they brought me the fleshy rump of a cockroach and a half grain of wheat for my breakfast. I had just finished eating when one of my teachers came to speak to me: "O my prince! You know that just now strange events transpire on the barren field to the north of our city. From the most recent reports of the scientific expedition conducted by the second finest scholar of our community, we are informed that the mysterious atmospheric conditions which caused a disagreement among all our experts have begun again. It is reported that these strange conditions have become a daily occurence. You must know that at midday when the sun radiates the greatest light, suddenly many parts of the brilliant sky are covered by a cluster of clouds. From time to time these clouds disappear but then return. Why? As you know, such natural events cannot be understood by logic and rational theories. For every situation, observation and experimentation are necessary. Countless experiments and observations have been made for years and as a result the mysteries of many natural events have been solved. In such a situation as this, eighty or ninety per cent of the time, our scholars can discover the solution, but as yet no one has managed to solve this strange puzzle. Today one of our teachers is delivering a lecture about his in-depth investigations into the problem. If it is convenient for you, please, let us go together to listen. The conference will take place on the field, and all the high school and university students will be gathering there."

On our way there we were met by many other ants; as we approached the strange field we formed a great crowd. The peculiar thing I was noticing was that I was equipped with the feelings, logic, and perception of both an ant and a human being. We entered the field. When I looked around with my ant's eyes, what I saw was quite bewildering and could be subject to much discussion and interpretation, but when I looked with a man's eyes, I saw clearly that we were on a wide avenue which was beautifully paved with flat Naples stones and lined by shops along both sides. Greatly amazed I began reasoning about the huge difference between the two perceptions. Just then one of our renowned naturalists began a lecture about the strange field phenomena: "Masters!" he began. "The thing that is most noteworthy is the regularity of the forms of these large cells and the canals between them. The cells are nearly flat and most of the cracks are filled with straight lines that have been almost perfectly arranged. Our experts have been unable to discover the reason for this orderly arrangement. Such artificiality doesn't exist in nature."

It was the sweetest moment of the lecture when suddenly a scream burst out among the hundreds of thousands of listeners. Although the sky was clear, at that very moment a terrible downpour had begun to drag off and drown thousands of ants. Rivers formed by this heavenly flood were carrying away and destroying thousands upon thousands of us. Everyone rushed in different directions. Though overcome for a moment by fear and horror, I soon felt a strong impulse arise in me to understand the reason for this peculiar flood. An intermittent downpour was continuing. When, with my human eyes, I surveyed this dreadful event I couldn't help being surprised and even amused. We were located on the side of the paved avenue referred to as "the strange field." A small carriage had stopped, and where we were standing the driver was sleeping happily while the horses ate their fodder from the sacks which hung around their necks. As if by agreement both horses had begun to urinate at the same time. This was the hot flood that had ruined the poor ants—nothing but the urine of horses.

I was among those who had died there. With great sorrow many ants busied themselves taking care of my body while others stood about mourning. Just opposite, some of the learned who had escaped were busy investigating the unusual flood.

Some time later one of the greatest naturalists discovered an explanation in a famous treatise in his library. It explained: "There is such a powerful magnetism and electricity in the strange field that from time to time this energy intensifies to such a degree that it blurs the air. Then even a very small accident can cause floods to discharge from the clouds." When I heard this declaration, the image of the tired horses eating their fodder and urinating appeared before my eyes. I laughed aloud and woke up. . . .

The Mirror was both laughing and playing a game that no one knew. At the same time he was murmuring:

The sun burns; the world turns.
A day comes; all are extinguished.
O man of skillful science,
Who is the cause; do you know?

CHAPTER THIRTEEN

Majnun With Layla[1]

*A*s soon as I could finish work, I would rush to bathe in the warm conversation of the Mirror. It had become almost an addiction for me. So, this afternoon, after work, I again ran to be with him. Seating himself under the shade of an ancient plane tree, the Mirror Dede spoke briefly, "My son! I'm feeling exuberant today. Let me play the ney."

He began to play, but it was really a mistake to call it a "ney," as it seemed to be the voice of all the sky and heavens singing together. It was not long before I passed beyond myself. . . .

I saw that I was the son of a wealthy nobleman within the City of Amal.[2] As I was an only son, my parents adored me. At the age of eighteen I was now a brave young man with thick eyebrows, and the people of the city were proud of my good looks and refined manners. Every morning I would ride my horse, wandering through the wide expanses beyond the city which were even more lovely than the central rose gardens. Sometimes I would hunt there for a while.

1. Majnun with Layla: Majnun was known as a lunatic of love. He was overcome by love for Layla. He was denied union with her and became a wandering ascetic. The fire of his love for her burned his soul until everything became Layla and he found his beloved in God.

2. City of Amal: the City of Longing, the beginning of the path of return to God.

Whenever I passed through the city streets, people would admire my appearance, remarking to each other, "How glorious he is! God is certainly the most gifted creator." Hoping to attract my attention, the most beautiful girls of the city would present themselves before me as I passed, but I was as proud as the hunting falcon I carried upon my arm. I would pretend not to even see them but, remaining aloof upon my horse, would just ride past. Little by little I began to feel a strange new fire in my heart, and though I could not point to the reason for this fire, it burned me deeply.

One day I found myself overcome by a deep sadness. I took my saz in hand and wept. In the days that followed, moaning and sadness became a habit for me; my face turned pale, and my interest in the world disappeared. Naturally the situation was not unknown to my parents. The story told among all the people of my city was that I had succumbed to a peculiar disease. A veil of sorrow enshrouded every-one. Our famous doctors prepared many different medicines; geomancers and healers all tried their skill, but day by day, my illness grew worse and worse.

At last, in a distant village, a hermit was located who was famous for his soothsaying and wisdom. My parents brought him to see me, but after closely consulting the medical wisdom of the centuries, he shook his head. He looked at his astrolabe, spoke with the stars, gath-ered jinns, then plunged into thought and was silent for a long while. At last, he spoke, "O master! Your son is in love. He is sick from love."

My poor father questioned him, "O honored master, who is he in love with?"

"Nobody! And this is the most destructive kind of love."

"O doctor! Tell us what we can do! What solution can we find? Even if the the only remedy is the sacrifice of our lives, we will not withhold it. We will give up anything, everything, but please let our beloved son be saved."

"Master, the love that is burning your son's heart is absolute love. An object must be found for this love, and then you must discover a way of extinguishing the fire of love with the life-restoring water of union. If this isn't done, he will certainly die."

My parents' joy was infinite. They now assumed that all that was required was a simple marriage. The most distinguished and beautiful young women of the city were introduced to me. My parents even waived their concern for equality of station and brought before me the most beautiful among the peasantry as well. But I loved none of them! I collapsed into bed. Day by day, my face grew paler, and my poor parents were overcome with worry.

I was no longer in any condition to sing or even to play my tanbur.[3] Thinking that perhaps it would help lessen my sorrow, my father gathered a group of the most perfect singers, both male and female, and instructed them to play the intricate, bittersweet pieces I had been known to enjoy.

One day, just after they had finished singing their laments, we heard the voice of a crier calling: "I am selling a closed coffer. Its value is a thousand pieces of gold. I do not know what is inside it; no one knows. The one who buys the coffer and the one who does not buy it will both be filled with regret."

My parents had heard the voice of the crier and, thinking that perhaps there was something inside to entertain me, immediately bought it. Curiosity, of which man can never totally free himself, caught hold of me despite my depression. I wanted to see what was inside the coffer. It had been months since I had expressed an interest in anything, so my parents were delighted and quickly placed the coffer at my side.

Countless keys were brought, but after trying for two days, I still had not found one that would fit. Because the coffer was exquisitely crafted, I didn't want to just break it. At last on the following day I managed to open it with difficulty. Only a single piece of paper and a picture were inside. First I looked at the piece of paper. On it was written: "The picture in this coffer is the picture of the Mirror of Union, Banu,[4] who is the daughter of Sultan Keramet, the Sultan of Miracles,

---

3. tanbur: a long necked lute especially used in the playing of Turkish classical music.

4. Banu: harvest; the golden one. The one who has found love within herself or himself has a golden aura.

the ruler of the City of Maksut[5] where all aims come to rest. A Zulaikha[6] is a worthless star in comparison with the radiant face of this young woman. Lovely birds are bewildered by her sweet voice; scholars shake in astonishment at the brilliance of her intelligence and her wisdom.

"At the moment Banu is fifteen-years-old, and all the young men of Maksut and the entire Jabilsa region have been ruined by love for her. O the poor man who sees this picture! Falling in love with its owner, you'll fall into difficulty. Know this well: the Mirror of Union is the most bewitching beauty of the universe. Since the age of twelve, she has destroyed thousands of gallant young men, young men in the spring of their lives. Thousands of young men have committed suicide; thousands have succumbed to tuberculosis and faded away. You, too, poor man, will join that group of martyrs. You won't be able to endure the despair of meeting with such a mirror, and you too will die."

After reading these dreadful words, without feeling any need to even think about it, I took the picture in my hand and looked at it. Why not? Death doesn't happen twice! Was I not already about to die from endless agony? They say that when I saw the picture I screamed and fainted. When I came to myself, I saw my parents weeping, distraught because I had lain still so long they thought I was dead. Now I, too, began to weep uncontrollably. Yet the more my tears flowed, the more like a tonic they became; the nightmare of sadness and grief was lessening.

That night, for the first time, I had the desire to eat. After dinner I drifted into a beautiful sleep softened with the sweetness of hope, the taste of which I had been deprived of for so long. I had found a focus for my love. With all my soul, with the burning love of my heart, I was immersed in love with the Mirror of Union, Banu.

In a short while I gathered myself together, and it was as if I had never fallen ill. My darling's picture was always in my hand, and her image was always in my heart. At night my beloved was at the center of all my thoughts, and it was she who enlivened my dreams with love.

5. Maksut: the goal; the place where desires come to an end. One strives so intensely that one dies. This is similar to the nothingness of Buddhism.
6. Zulaikha: the wife of Potiphar who was known for her phenomenal beauty.

At last I decided what I must do and went to my parents' room and respectfully kissed their hands. Then I spoke: "O dear parents, cause of my life! I must go in search of my beloved; I must attain union with her. If I am unable to do so, I will surely die. I am determined to go to the city of Maksut, in the Jabilsa region."

At these words of mine, my father and mother looked at each other in astonishment, but after conferring briefly, they recognized that it would be useless to try to change my mind. Immediately they invited the most experienced, virtuous, and wise people of the city to gather in order to discuss the situation. My parents told them of my determination and requested their opinions.

An esteemed person among them asked permission to speak. "In order to bring forth an idea about this matter one has to know the Jabilsa region and the City of Maksut, and one has to understand where it is. As I have only just heard about this city now for the first time, I wonder if perhaps its existence is news to the others of this assembly as well."

The great ones who had gathered agreed with him and said that they had never before heard of such a place either. After some discussion they decided to approach the soothsayer hermit who had been able to diagnose my love. He was considered the wisest among us. So once again the soothsayer was brought to our home, and when my determination was explained to him, he thought for a while and then spoke, "The City of Maksut is in the region of Jabilsa, far to the west. It lies further west than any other city, in the same way that our city, Amal, is the furthest east. If one were fast enough, one could arrive there in a year's time."

My parents again assembled the wise ones of our city to consider and discuss the soothsayer's words. At last they came to the conclusion that it was impossible to change my mind and a common decision was made: I would go to Maksut, and fifteen of our most faithful servants would accompany me. For about twenty days we busied ourselves choosing suitable presents for Sultan Keramet and his wife. We also had a sedan chair prepared for the honored soothsayer so that he could accompany me.

At last, one morning after a very sad farewell with my parents, at the moment deemed most auspicious by the astrologers, we set out. My relatives and many of the city's people accompanied us to the outskirts of our city and prayed for our safety and well-being. One of the saints read a beautiful prayer for our success. Our journey had begun.

After experiencing many difficulties during the course of the year that followed—troubles which would be tiresome to relate—we at last had the good fortune to reach the Jabilsa region and the city of Maksut. We went to a large caravanserai inside the city. Because the city's grapevine was quite efficient, everyone already knew about our arrival from the Far East, and a large crowd of people hurried to meet us. Those to whom we told the reason for our visit would shake their heads in agitation and express their sorrow.

After resting for ten days, the soothsayer and I approached the sultan's palace. At last we were accepted into his presence. We presented our gifts, and he asked us the reason for our visit. When we told him, he frowned and immediately ordered an assembly of the state vizirs and ministers.

When we explained our intentions to them, their faces filled with sorrow and pity. The sultan spoke: "My son! The life of my daughter Banu, the Mirror of Union, is given to me with one condition: I must never interfere with her concerning her marriage. But let me say this much: thousands who have come have been ruined, thousands killed for the sake of this girl. She asks a few questions of every seeker. Ruin comes to those who cannot answer. She will marry no one except he who can answer her questions. So far not one of the thousands of young men has ever been able to do so. I do not wish such a fine young man as you to be destroyed like the others. I beg of you, come, give up this unlucky love."

After the sultan had finished, the ministers and vizirs also asked permission to speak and tried to persuade me to give up my intention. I continued to insist and finally told them that I wished to be tested as soon as possible and explained that I had contemplated the matter long enough. I was ready to either attain my wish or be destroyed in the effort.

After a short discussion the vizirs told me to return to the palace the following day. I returned to my quarters and waited without sleeping. At last morning came, and together with the soothsayer, I returned to the palace. We were led into a large, magnificently decorated hall. A huge curtain divided it in half. I was seated on an armchair just in front of the middle of the curtain, and the old soothsayer took his place next to me. The viziers, ministers, and other notables of the country were seated near us in other armchairs, and a huge crowd of people filled the remainder of the hall.

The rustling of silk dresses and the fragrance of sweet scents that can intoxicate men informed us that the Mirror of Union and those accompanying her were entering the hall. After some time the curtain was removed. Banu was seated upon a high throne, her face veiled. Hundreds of attendants had gathered around her; they stood in great respectfulness, their hands crossed over their chests.

The girl examined me attentively for a long time from behind her veil. It seemed as if she was afraid to say a word, but at last with a voice that was beyond comparison with any music or sound, she began to speak melodiously: "O young man! Come, give up this love. Nobody could answer these questions. Those who have the power to answer are already content in their hearts because they are already in union with me. Those who have desire for me will never be able to answer what I ask."

"O Banu! When I left my homeland, I swore, 'Either the beloved or death.' O Mirror of Union! I cannot live without you."

"O young man, what a pity! If it were possible for me to marry you without any conditions, I would. But unfortunately it is not possible, because as a result of our union both of us would disappear."

"O Banu! Don't make me despair; have mercy! Ask your questions."

She sighed deeply.

"Listen very carefully, young man! First, has *alif*[7] come out of the dot or has the dot come out of *alif*? Second, when did it happen? Third, can you demonstrate and prove that *alif* and the dot are one?"

7. *alif*: the first letter of the Arabic alphabet ا . The second letter, *b* ب is the first letter which uses a dot.

After asking these questions, she removed her veil. When I beheld her extraordinary face, I could not bear the burning pleasure of seeing her; with a cry of "God is Most Great," I fainted. . . .

When I opened my eyes, the Mirror Father was smiling upon me. Full of joy, he spoke:

"*Alif ustin* [e], *alif esre* [i], *alif otre* [u].[8] Well, lots more questions! How does it happen that *alif* accepts movement? Can the matter be solved by calling *alif* '*hamze*'?[9] O my God! What a difficult thing this *alif-ba* problem is. There are lots of teachers of reading and writing, but not one of them knows *alif-ba*."

After chatting a while longer, having decided to meet again the next day, we said goodbye to each other, and I took my leave of the Mirror Dede.

8. *Alif ustin* . . . : Each of the Ottoman Turkish vowels is structured around the letter *alif*. According to those who believe in the unity of God, the origin of every letter is *alif*, symbolizing this unity; within every letter there is an *alif*.

9. *hamze*: the glottal stop indicator in the Arabic alphabet; it modifies the pronunciation of *alif*.

CHAPTER FOURTEEN

The Lunatics without Layla

*A*s we had agreed, we met again towards evening the next day. The Mirror placed his coffee pot on the alcohol burner, and we were soon chatting and drinking our coffee. . . .

Today's dream began where it had been interrupted the day before. I had fainted, and immediately afterwards Banu had sighed deeply and also fainted. They had taken her to the palace and me to my residence. When I came to myself the soothsayer was standing over me, gazing sadly into my face. I decided that if I could not answer the questions I would commit suicide.

I went over the questions with the soothsayer and asked him how we could possibly answer them. He said, "My son, only those who live in the Valley of Madness know the answers to these questions."

"All right, then, where is this valley?"

"Everywhere."

"I don't understand."

"There is no absolute place called 'the Valley of Madness.' In this world, The Valley of Madness is everywhere."

"Well, how do we find such a place?"

"Nothing is easier. We will make the necessary preparations and set out tomorrow."

The next day, our journey began. We searched through numerous towns and cities for three months but were unable to find a place that resembled the Valley of Madness. I began to be discouraged.

At last we arrived at the outskirts of a very great city, but as it was late, the gates of the citadel were already closed. We pitched our tent near the cemetery adjacent to the city walls and, fatigued by travel, soon fell asleep. I awoke quite early. By the time the soothsayer and I were drinking our coffee, dawn had broken. Just then, from the cemetery we heard laughter.

The soothsayer spoke, "There are two spaceless places which are the aim. One is the Valley of Astonishment; the other is the Valley of Madness!" He smiled as he continued. "My son, here we have found the Valley of Madness. Stand up; let's go visit its inhabitants."

We went into the cemetery. Seven people were seated in a circle atop one grave. One of them, who seemed to be stirred by the laughter and a poem which had just been recited, asked, "What is it? Is it the call to prayer?"

The soothsayer explained to me that this was one of the "astonished ones."

Another one of them replied to the first, "No hasty assumptions or doubt can enter our territory. Neither knowledge, nor intellect, nor sciences exist."

When another one heard this, he replied, "Is the imam[1] reciting the Quranic chapter on the unbelievers, Surah Kafirun?"[2]

Another said, "I guess a nightingale is singing."

Yet another said, "What did you say? Has the coffee pot boiled over?"

And another, "It must be the sound of the waves."

1. imam: a moslem religious leader usually affiliated with a particular mosque. The one who is responsible for leading prayers, delivering the Friday sermon, and arranging religious instruction.
2. Surah Kafirun: Surah CIX, "Surah of the Unbelievers" which defines the appropriate attitude towards those who reject faith: we must not compromise when it comes to truth, but there is no need to persecute anyone because of a difference of faith.

The last one spoke, "I think the halvah seller is calling. Let's buy some. In every state Ferihun[3] makes himself a pleasure; he has written the sign of Kulli Hizbin[4] upon his seal."

One began to shout, "Neither this, nor that!"

Then they all fell silent. The soothsayer and I approached one of them and in a respectful manner attempted to kiss his hand. He laughed and said: "If you wish to kiss someone, go and kiss Hacer-i Esved,[5] the black stone of the Kaaba. In order to kiss nothingness, no reputation is necessary. Can the soul ever be embraced with finite words? To kiss the lip of the heart, the soul is necessary."

We approached another one, but as soon as I said, "O sage of knowledge, our petitions. . ." he burst into laughter and said: "For naming the blind 'wise,' the seer was called 'crazy.' Science has validated so many myths; yet his science and wisdom were called 'imaginary.'"

We tried to approach a third person, explaining the reason for our visit and why we wished his help. All the while I was asking for his help, he remained still, like the others, but as soon as I stopped speaking and waited for his answer, he began: "Is it raining? So! There is one who wants, one who does not want. There is one who wants and does not want; there is also one who neither wants nor does not

3. Ferihun: joyousness. This refers to the end of the 53rd verse of Surah Muminum (Surah XXIII): "They have torn their unity apart into sects, each group delighting in that which they possess [their own way and beliefs]."

4. Kulli Hizbin: each sect. This also refers to the 53rd verse of Surah Muminum: each group trusts its own religion, its own sect and believers.

5. Hacer-i Esved: the holy black stone in the Kaaba; one and one half meters high at the corner, it is egg-shaped with light yellow and red veins and has a diameter of thirty centimeters. It is said that this stone was accepted as holy before the advent of Islam and that it was placed by Abraham into the foundations of the Kaaba which were raised by Abraham and Ishmael. According to one tradition the black stone was given to Adam upon his expulsion from paradise in order that he might obtain forgiveness for his sins. Some say that it was found among the foundation stones while the Kaaba was being built. Another tradition tells that it was found within the Well of Zam Zam. The Kaaba is the focal point of prayer for all Muslims, and pilgrimage to the Kaaba is one of the sacred duties. Each Muslim who makes the pilgrimage circumambulates the Kaaba seven times and kisses the black stone during the process. Damaged many times during its history, the Kaaba was most recently rebuilt in 605 (according to the Western calendar), and the stone was placed in the eastern corner under the direction of Muhammad.

want. And what does 'is' mean?"

We could see that we would not be able to communicate with them and so we moved over into a corner where the soothsayer said, "Let's be patient and watch."

After a while one of them approached us, and I thought, "Well, now we will be able to speak," and I went to meet him.

"Welcome, master," I said.

"Oh, I could not 'come well.'" he said.

"My master, your name?" I asked.

"It changes every minute," he replied.

"My master, then who are you?"

"How do I know? If I knew would I be a cook here?"

I had had enough, but the soothsayer recommended patience. "They must be informed of our wish and our intention. Let's wait and see. We will stay here and undergo austerities for a few days and see what time reveals."

We did what was necessary. I had already lost my appetite, so a few olives in twenty-four hours were enough for me. Thirty-nine days passed while we waited. Exactly on the fortieth day one of the crazy ones called to one of the astonished. They sat down on the ground facing each other, and the rest formed a crescent around them. For a time all of them passed beyond themselves, diving into their own inner worlds. But after a while the crazy one and the astonished one began speaking.

First the crazy one spoke, "O, astonished one! You have read; you have written; and you have realized its meaning also. How did you realize the Meaning?"

The astonished one answered, "With alif/ba."

"What does 'the Meaning' mean?"

"One becoming two and two becoming one."

"What is the name of this?"

"The Word of Oneness."[6]

"How can one be united? Is it possible to divide it, or is it compound?"

6. the Word of Oneness (*Kalimat-i Tawhid*): "*La illaha il Allah*"; The Islamic attestation to the unity of God: "There is no reality, no god but God."

"No! One is simple and without defect. It cannot be divided either."

"Then how does one become two? And why are there two lines in oneness?"

"One of the two lines is affirmation; the other is negation. The existence of negation is the shadow of affirmation. For this reason the truth of the two lines is one. If there were only one line, then there could be duality."

"Oh! What is all this called?"

"It has three names: 'the Art of Creation,' 'the Play of Appearance,' and 'the Plays of Oneness.'"

"When did this happen?"

"Time is an aspect related to the negation side. There is no time in the body; there is only the moment!"

"Alright, what is that you call the 'moment'?"

"It is absolute negation. Absolute nothingness is the affirmation of timelessness and absolute time in separation."

"What does 'alif/ba' mean?"

"The phenomena of universes. . . ."

"Which letter is the origin?"

"*Alif*!"

"The origin of what? Of the body or of the phenomena?"

"It cannot be of the body. Of the phenomena."

"What is the origin of *alif*?"

"The dot!"

"Do you accept *alif* or the dot as the bodies?"

"The dot! The body speaks with the silent *alif*."

"Oh! This means that there are two kinds of bodies?"

"No! *Alif* and the dot are one."

"Then how did *alif* happen to be?"

"This is a problem. Words cannot contain it!"

"Give an example!"

"There can be no equal or anything similar or opposite to it."

"Then show me a model!"

"The example can be realized only by those who are free from the restriction of time and space."

"What is the example?"

"The bee."

"What does the bee make?"

"Honey, in order that it may be loved."

"And what else does it do?"

"It makes wax, in order to inform."

With limitless joy, the crazy one exclaimed, "May God be blessed, O crown of the wise! The Valley of Astonishment is yours; the Valley of the Mad is yours, too. I have one last question. Show us an example!"

I became increasingly astonished with each passing moment as the questions of the Mirror of Union, Banu, were completely solved by this dialogue. Now neither Banu nor any other form remained in my heart; the Mirror of Union had become my heart. My inside was my outside before, but now my outside was my inside. Now I was "in love" in the real sense of the word. I was in union with myself.

While I was in this state, the astonished one took a piece of wax out of his pocket. Showing it to those who were around him, he spoke, "O community! That is the dot."

Then, heating the wax with his breath, he lengthened it and said, "That is *alif*."

Then the crazy one stood up and said, "Tell us! Does *alif* have another name!"

The astonished one replied, "Yes, it does, but let me say it in your ear."

He approached the crazy one and whispered a few things. They embraced each other, and then turning toward me, the crazy one spoke, "O, young man! Now you have become Majnun without Layla, because Majnun became Layla. If Layla is also removed from between, then you can know the other name of *alif* that was whispered into my ear. . . ."

Infused with joy, I opened my eyes. The Mirror, the great one, was singing with his magnificently touching voice, "O Majnun, with the artful play of majesty, Layla has become the Lord."

CHAPTER FIFTEEN

The Chain Embellished with Precious Stones:

The Lot of the Universe

*I*t was a beautiful day. The Mirror Dede and I were sitting together; the coffee pot was on the fire as usual. Even before I had finished my sweet coffee, this day's vision began. . . .

I was flying. Ordinarily I couldn't stand the thought of flying, even in my dreams, so this imaginary flying was exhausting and bewildering to me. The strange thing was that I wasn't flying straight forward but continually upward. Planets and suns completely disappeared before my eyes. At last I came to a place where I was able to stop; I could stand in this space like a balloon that had reached the highest possible elevation.

After resting for a while, I began flying again, towards the right this time. I encountered someone who was also flying somewhat aimlessly as I was. I greeted him, and he stopped and inquired who I was. I answered and added that I seemed to have no will of my own and no knowledge of how I had risen to that place. He replied, "This is the

Intermediate Universe.[1] I am Pythagoras."

"Pythagoras? The famous Pythagoras, the philosopher Pythagoras?"

"Yes."

"O master, how happy that makes me! What an honor! To meet a great master like you is such a blessing for someone like me who has thousands of problems."

"My son, this is not the world. Here there is no need for lying. Don't keep calling me 'great master.' As if my hard work in the world were not enough, for centuries I have been thinking about the same problem here. I know that the essence of phenomena is oneness, because the origin of all numbers is one. From another point of view, the universe means harmony. But there are problems that I cannot solve. I want to write and think, but what can one do? In this strange emptiness, there is neither a board to write on nor anything to write with. Do you have some paper and a pen with you?"

His explanation bewildered me. I took my leave of this master who had not been able to rid himself of thought or anxiety. After a while I came across another shadow. I greeted him, but before he returned my greeting, he asked, "Have you seen my apprentice Plato and his apprentice Aristotle?"

Surprised by his question, I inquired, "Why do you want them?"

He replied, "Here, there are no sophists to ridicule or to entrap. I am quite bored. If I could find our Plato and our Aristotle, I would get them to argue with each other and would entertain myself by listening to their debate.

From the way he spoke I understood that this person was the great philosopher Socrates. He flew off leaving me to my own boredom within this vast field of loneliness. As I was about to wander on, a beautiful shadow approached me. With harmonious pronunciation he began to speak poetic words.

"Yes," he said, "those we saw and knew in the world were all the dim images and memories of the higher universe and the truth which our spirits saw there."

---

1. Intermediate Universe: the intermediate state of the soul after death and before judgment; the grave.

I asked, "Who are you, sir?"

"I am Plato!"

"I am your humble servant, but I really don't see any truth here. On the contrary, all I know and see here are but the memories of what I saw and knew in the world."

"That is because this is not the High Universe. Though we are not restricted here as we were on earth, still we are not pure spirits. On earth we had bodies. Here also we have a body, but it is subtle, not solid. Therefore, what we see and know in the Intermediate Universe are the memories of memories."

"But why do we cling to this emptiness called the 'Intermediate Universe'; why do we stay here? Why don't we go on to those places you describe as the 'High Universe'?"

"This is the problem which I have been thinking about and working diligently on for two thousand years. Why are we obliged to dwell in this intermediate space? If you ever discover the answer, please come and tell me about it. My students are waiting; I am going now to give them a lesson. Have a nice time. Good-bye."

"O, philosopher! For God's sake, stay awhile! Are there lessons exchanged here in the Intermediate Universe, as well?"

"If there were not such entertainments, one would go to pieces from boredom. And why should I hide it? I find happiness in answering all the objections and criticisms my pupil Aristotle presents."

Plato left. I was astonished that I still was not free of difficulties, restrictions, ambitions, and reactions here in this Intermediate Universe. I opened my eyes. . . .

The great Mirror was speaking: "There is neither bird, nor birds, but within a single pleasure this one exists and that one does as well. In spite of this, my son, perhaps you are nauseated. Let me prepare some coffee for you."

I drank the coffee, and immediately I envisioned myself flying again. . . .

Many shadows flew around me, and I flew aimlessly among them. After some time, we gathered together, and it became apparent that these were writers of all sorts, including writers of ethics, poetry, and medicine. I joined in their conversation. Although our ideas about this space in which we were flying were similar, none of us could formulate a really correct statement or come up with a solution to the problem of our existence here. We continued to fly and to talk, deepening our conversation as we flew. The one who was the most outspoken was the writer on ethics. Voices of both agreement and dissent were heard around him. Just then, one of the famous literary men, whose name I later learned was Chata, began to say something interesting: "My dear moralist! Here you are making another mistake and slandering all of us. I assure you that with a few changes your works will be accepted by people and will be viewed as worthy of being printed hundreds of times. Your words could be accepted by theaters and be produced on stage, as an encouragement for the new generation. Yes, these works could be immortalized."

Everyone listened in bewilderment. As he continued, he became quite exuberant and excited: "Yes, my dear ones, yes. Just think. Today's situation is worthy of consideration. Almost no subject remains that has not been examined and written about; mentalities have shifted, and in every area strange changes have occurred. Things thought to be new or quaint in the old days are seen as neither by the current generation. In every arena of life, people have invented odd phenomena—I don't know whether to call them novelties or insanities. The most serious works are laughed at by this new generation. Isn't it true that people now find it entertaining to view life as a machine, the spirit as an illusion, and conscience as an unfortunate inheritance—and to mock at scholars who describe the meaning of life with words such as 'self-sacrifice' and 'mission'? So, honored teacher! O moralist! With your outstanding works, before long you will be revered as the most famous comedy writer of the age!"

While this lecture was taking place we had approached a space where we now stopped flying. I saw that the moralist had an important load of knowledge, a sack of manuscripts of printed works on his back. Either from the exertion of flying or from delivering the lecture or for some other unknown reason, he now fell to the ground with a "pat." We all crowded around him. One of our flying friends, Doctor Pataban, a specialist in treating those who crash to the ground, examined the moralist. "My God! His stomach is empty; there is nothing inside it to digest. He has fainted because his stomach is digesting itself."

The insipid conversation between these writers and literary men propelled me to join a different group of people. Among this other group, two were speaking: "There is no equality in breathing the air. In this universe in which one pays a tax on everything, there is still no tax on air. Can you think of anything stranger than this?"

"My dear, you speak so beautifully. One should suggest such a tax. The income would be at least a few hundred million lira."

I removed myself from this seemingly pointless conversation as well. A neatly-dressed person was standing nearby. He was also a writer, and we began to talk a bit. He scolded me, telling me that unlike my relative who spent his time writing useful works, I had wasted my life. He asked whether I had written at least one complete work this year. I told him that I had tried, but that it was not the right time to read it, as it was covered with dust. After casting a mocking smile at me, he said: "Look, I wrote something perfect this year, but what use will it be if I tell you the name of it? Nothing could be understood in that way. Don't forget: science is not a worthy thing in itself. It is only of value if it makes work easier for those who know about work. Scholars who are not aware of this truth might be admired by the ignorant, but they cannot save themselves from their own emptiness forever. Great applause and appreciation without monetary compensation have little worth other than as consolation for the destitute."

A large field was in front of me; people had gathered there in groups. As I had become very curious about this Intermediate Universe, I said to the writer, "Let's see what's going on over there." I flew and walked until I reached an open place. In the center of the open area a high platform had been erected, and in the middle of it, a taffy-seller's whirligig had been set up. While I was looking at it, trying to determine what it was for, a terrible hunchback arrived. He sat down on the edge of the whirligig. Lumps bulged out on his front and on his back such as I had never seen in all my life. The strange thing was that the front lump was transparent so that I could see the inside which was like a merchant's shop with various kinds of goods displayed. My vision had changed in an unusual way so that I could also perceive the inside of the huge lump as resembling a market larger than the court-yard of the main mosque in Jerusalem,[2] composed of countless rooms. I watched in amazement.

Just then a man was brought forward, led by the hands—I could see that he was blind—and was seated beside the whirligig as well. Mean-while the moralist, the crowd of literary men, and Doctor Pataban had arrived. Someone near me was whispering, "This hunchback is destiny, and the blind man is fortune."

We all moved into a circle around the whirligig. The blind man began spinning it. The hunchback who still was sitting upon it and was also helping to whirl it at the same time began throwing things outward at the crowd. Those nearby scrambled to snatch them up, but the odd thing was that before anyone could reach for anything, his lot would fall on his head. Group by group, we moved forward. Soon it was the turn of the writers and the literary men to circle close. I was in a position between the bureaucrats and the writers. There were so many bureaucrats that to make sure I would get my share I insinu-ated myself into the smaller circle of writers. By a strange coincidence the teacher of ethics now happened to be on my left. The terrible hunchback continued to throw something at each person. When it was my turn to receive, something heavy hit me in the head and knocked me down. As I fell over, the teacher of ethics, Chat, who was already very weak, fell down, too. When the confusion subsided, the first thing I did was to look to see what had been given to me that had knocked me over with such force. O my God! It was a large basket of rotten tomatoes. Some of the split tomatoes had smeared across my head, face, and eyes. As I looked around through this sauce—which was appar-ently my destined lot—something even stranger caught my eye. I saw that the ethics teacher had been knocked down, not by my fall but by a basket of eggs. As he was very weak, he had not been able to catch it and almost all of the eggs had been broken, and now a slippery polish

2. the main mosque in Jerusalem: *Masjid-i Aksa*; the holy house in Jerusalem which marks the location of Solomon's temple and the spot where Muhammad as-cended during his *miraj*, his night journey towards God.

covered him so that he looked like an egg-coated piece of filet of sole just ready for the frying pan. His Honor, Chat, who was an extremely resigned person, was attempting to eat the slimy egg dripping off his head by gathering it meticulously with his fingers. Forgetting that I myself was smeared with rotten tomatoes, I burst into laughter at his predicament. With great seriousness, this teacher of ethics was muttering to himself, "Almost a thousand eggs! At least if they hadn't been broken, I could have made my living off them for a year and could have had printed at least three or maybe five of my unpublished works, which I have been carrying around on my back for all these years."

Just then the neatly-dressed person, who had told me that nothing could be understood by the title of his work, came over to us with a purse of gold in his hand. When he saw Chat eating the egg goo with his fingers and saw me laughing, he said: "How foolish you are! When there is a way of deriving benefit from anything in the world, you are doing just the opposite. I'm sure that even if I were to give you this purse of gold in my hand, you wouldn't know how to spend it. Why don't you lick each other's faces so that at least you will have eaten eggs with tomatoes. Go on! Don't wait. Don't waste time."

The ethics writer immediately put his arms around my neck and with his thin, hard tongue, that from weakness and undernourishment had toughened to resemble the nose of a South American anteater, he began to lick my face. As this abrasive catlike tongue touched my skin, it tickled me so much that rather than being able to lick the egg off his face, I found myself incapacitated from laughter. I tried to extricate myself from his wiry but firmly locked arms; with our hands around each others throats, we fell down on the ground again. At last after some time had passed, I managed to untangle myself.

I opened my eyes. . . .

The Magnificent Mirror, with a plate in his hand, was coming towards me from the gate of the cemetery. Smiling, he was speaking to himself:

The Universe is a sea.
You are a ship.
Your intellect is the sail.

117

Your ideas are the rudder.
So, let me see you!
Free yourself. . . .

He put the plate in front of me and sat down. He took some bread out of the basket and handed it to me. In the plate was tomato salad garnished with an egg. I remembered the things I had seen in the Intermediate Universe. The Mirror smiled again.

"With one difference, it is so; but is it so if the difference is thrown away? Don't think about it too much. It's a salad prepared with some of the tomatoes that weren't crushed and with some of the eggs which didn't break. Go ahead, spoon it out! Whatever your lot is, it will come out in your spoon. Please help yourself. The moment is again this moment, my son!"

CHAPTER SIXTEEN

The Eternal Retirement of the Mirror

I was feeling a strange tastelessness and lack of clarity in my soul. Before finishing work I stopped by to see the Mirror. He smiled when he saw me, but his face held a new expression.

"So, my son, the time has come for me to emigrate. May God be your helper and your guide! Would you mind stopping by here tomorrow morning? I am leaving you a pouch and its contents as a souvenir. Keep me in your heart always so that I may be with you every moment. As he spoke and I began to realize the meaning of his words, I couldn't help crying.

The Mirror's eyes also filled with tears, and he pressed me to his chest.

"What can one do, my son! Coming and going belong to this universe. Why get caught up in outward appearances? Every day He is at work. We cannot be outside of God's order."

I remained with him until quite late. The hours flew. Was it an invisible lightning? I don't know. Finally in the darkness of the night, we parted, both quite sad.

I couldn't sleep at all. Before dawn I returned to the cemetery. A pleasant early morning breeze was blowing, carrying a holy sound into even the most depressed hearts. I was extremely sad and afraid. The Great Mirror of pure light was lying with his arms crossed over his chest under the terebinth tree which he had always loved. He was smiling and relaxed as if he were dreaming a beautiful dream. I approached, full of longing and love. My tears washed over his blessed hands as I wept and wept, unaware of the passing of time. My heart could not let go to make the preparations for the final human task, but at last I stood up.

I gathered a small group of people whom The Mirror loved, and together we buried him under the terebinth tree. Until evening an uneasy listlessness gnawed my soul, and I wandered about aimlessly.

My night passed in thoughts and memories. The following morning, I remembered the souvenir. Still heavy with grief, I entered the Mirror Dede's hut. A small leather saddle bag was waiting for me. I opened it and discovered one large and two small coffee pots, four or five cups, about a hundred grams of sugar and coffee, and a hand written Qur'an together with a small pocket notebook.

Before long, I had the hut restored. From then on I passed time there whenever I was free from worldly occupations.

If you were to look through the entries in his pocket notebook, you would appreciate the Mirror Dede's beautifully legible handwriting. This notebook contained quite a number of poems and stories filled with wisdom; among them are some which could be of use to you, so I offer them here.

***

Stories from the Notebook
of the Mirror Dede

CHAPTER SEVENTEEN

Happiness

*E*very human being, every sentient creature, including even the lowest of animals, begins to search for happiness from the moment it feels the impulse of life. This law is so constant that, even if every other natural law were to change, this tendency would probably remain the same. Most creatures, because their wants, pleasures, and thoughts are within limits, find some degree of happiness. Yet it is the ordinary human being, who, though his capacity for happiness is great, does not really understand the true nature of the happiness he seeks and so seldom finds it. He or she never envisions a limit for the attainment of happiness. Unfortunately, due to this never ending aspiration, there are even some happy people who develop the opinion that they aren't happy and so end up making a hell out of their fleeting lives. What an enigma the human being is! Is it a necessity of creation that human beings should be so strange? People obtain many things; yet the more they possess, the more ambitious they become.

What is happiness? Few really know. Perhaps only the crazy ones, those oblivious to the turmoil of life, might be considered happy.

Please pay attention for a moment. One may compare a city to a theater and its inhabitants to actors. Not long ago I was in a city where due to the necessities of living I was in contact with most of the population. I observed many people. Because almost all of them were afflicted by real or imagined deficiencies, they were unhappy. In that crowded place, three personalities caught my attention. Two of them were quite odd.

One of these was the imam of the district in which I was living. He was well-educated and had even gone to Al-Azhar University[1] in Cairo. Nevertheless, he was loquacious, flagrantly wealthy, and given to imitating celebrities. Though he was boastful and extremely conservative, he was highly esteemed and influential. He would continually preach that the end of time had arrived, that faith and conviction had weakened, and that doomsday was at hand. He saw fault in *everyone* but himself and would never accept the purity of anyone else's prayers or ablutions. He could not see that anyone else was truly following the rules of the religion with the proper fear of God. This imam could have been quite content with what he already had, but instead, while publicly abstemious, his private search for happiness and pleasure led him to involvement in various immoral activities. He began to practise usury, lending money to peasants secretly, awaiting the interest. Though the eating of pork was forbidden, he could swallow a whole pig, tail and all, when necessary. He gave sermons about surrendering oneself to unfortunate destiny and yet would quickly cover his ears at the sound of thunder. He spent more and more of his time pursuing secret, illicit entertainments which had brought him face to face with unnecessary and unpleasant situations.

Another odd personality was the shaikh[2] of a local *tekke*.[3] He lived luxuriously with the regular income of this *tekke* which he had inherited from his father. He knew many stories about the saints and prophets and could defend himself from many false beliefs and ways of think-

1. Al-Azhar University: the oldest Islamic university, founded in the ninth century in Cairo.
2. shaikh: a venerated leader, especially of a mystical order. Originally used as a title of respect for the chief of an Arab tribe; derived from *shakha*, to grow old.
3. *tekke*: dervish center, a building or cluster of buildings where dervishes might live while undergoing training and where ceremonies were held.

ing. He knew the rules of many rituals, had important dreams all the time, and could gather and bind jinns and elemental forces. However, his fear of the jinns was so great he wouldn't even go to the bathroom at night without his wife accompanying him. He sometimes attended to his family's needs, and sometimes not. He was a simple, foolish, and lazy man. With just a few changes he could have become quite balanced and more helpful to those around him; yet he persisted in his useless behavior and so continued to suffer.

It's the third person whom I really want to tell you about. According to my observations, he is the one who was actually content and who to a certain extent had succeeded in creating a happy family. It was during some of my excursions through the city, that a carpenter named Hamdun, who lived quite near me, caught my attention. He was about forty-years-old, and from his countenance and the way he moved, it was easy to see that he was strong and healthy. Whenever I passed by, we would greet each other, and he always seemed full of joy.

One day with the freedom due a holy fool, I took a seat in the corner of his shop. He welcomed me with respect and happiness and sent his youngest apprentice to order some coffee. Brother Hamdun returned to planing a piece of wood. "Dede, a carpenter must not spend his time idly talking. These three apprentices are my sons, and I don't wish to be a bad example for them. So, if you will excuse me, I will work while we talk."

Two young men with arms like wrestlers, one about twenty, the other perhaps sixteen, were busy at their work nearby. Further inside the shop, a plump boy of about nine, who had just returned with the coffee, was attempting to separate the sawdust from the woodchips and put them into a sack. As I watched, I drank my coffee. "Brother Hamdun," I remarked, "so these, may God bless them, are your sons?"

"Yes, all three of them. The oldest, my first child, is almost twenty. He has already become one of the most skillful and hard-working master carpenters in the region. He even learned new skills on his own, like the carving of olive wood which I myself don't know. Soon he will be better at it than the most experienced carvers in the city. At present he earns one silver coin a day."

"Oh! From whom does he get his wages?"

"From whom would he get them? From me. Suppose I didn't have a son and hired a master craftsman to work with me. Wouldn't a master craftsman receive a silver coin a day? Instead of hiring someone from the outside, I chose to employ my own sons."

Astonished, I asked, "Does a father give daily pay to his sons?"

"Of course! If a boy doesn't receive daily wages from his father who employs him, how is he going to learn about the value of working? He will probably become lazy. With no real value given to his efforts, he will tend to neglect things. He'll feel that his father is supplying him with shelter in exchange for his work, and not simply because he is a part of the family. As a result he loses his virtue. Instead, working together could be a useful opportunity for a child to learn how to earn money and understand its value. This is why I pay my sons daily wages. My second son receives ten kurush now, but in three days, when the new week begins, he graduates to master workman status, and I will be raising his pay to fifteen kurush. My youngest son still receives twenty para, the same amount that I first earned from my late master. He is hard-working and very enterprising, and may well surpass his brothers one day. Though he really deserves a kurush now, I have not increased his wages because from hurry and carelessness he has cut his hand twice. I don't appreciate careless people, but if he doesn't cut his hand again, he will soon deserve a kurush a day."

"This must mean that they also share the household expenses?"

"How could that be?" Hamdun replied, "Let's suppose that I didn't have any sons. Would my master craftsman and apprentices share my household expenses? Or let's suppose that like many others, my sons are incapable of earning money for themselves. How could they share my expenses? Instead, my sons save what they earn. Besides his wages, my oldest son has a considerable amount of capital which I put aside for him long ago. Because he adds his wages to it, it will soon be almost equal to my capital. Before long, I'll help him open a proper workshop of his own or make him a partner in mine, and then perhaps marriage will follow so that our home may be filled with the joys

125

of grandchildren. And similarly with my second son, and the third, according to their wishes."

"Brother, this means that you are rather rich, aren't you?"

Hamdun called to his sons, "Raise your arms, please." The boys raised their arms. "Look, Mirror Dede, don't you agree that these eight arms are riches? As I said, I finished setting aside my oldest son's initial capital a long time ago. Soon I will complete my second son's also. Dede, do you know that I was married at the age of twenty? At that time my daily wages were seven kurush. My oldest son was born the following year. My late master, Haji Murteza, raised my daily wages to fifteen kurush. He showed me a way. From that day I began to save: sixty para [one and a half kurush] for my son's money, as well as three kurush for the time when I won't be able to work due to sickness, ten para for the clothing expenses of poor children on holidays, ten para as alms, three kurush to gather into capital, two kurush for our house rent, et cetera. The five kurush remaining was enough for us to live on."

I replied, "I'm astonished by this orderly life. This means your master Haji Murteza was a very good man."

The carpenter's eyes filled with tears, "May the grace of God be upon him. Whatever I have is under his auspices."

"May God increase your happiness. May God grant health and a long life for your wife and your sons," I responded.

This prayer of mine made the carpenter very happy. First his youngest and then the other sons came over and kissed my hand. I became so happy at their situation that my eyes, which for a long time hadn't had sufficient reason to weep, either out of sadness or sweetness, now filled with tears.

"Tell me more about the life you live," I said.

"We get up very early in the morning. Whether it is summer or winter, we wash our faces with cold water, and then young or old, we each drink a cup of coffee. After chatting together for a while, we take the pot that was simmered earlier by my wife to the table and drink some soup. Then my sons and I leave and walk to the workshop. On the way one of us goes off to do the necessary household shopping for the day, takes it home, and meets the others at the workshop. When we are all together again, I discuss the work of the day with my sons, and we all set about our tasks. Around noon, when we get hungry, the youngest goes home and brings our meal, and we have a nice lunch. After lunch I order coffee from the nearby café and get a newspaper. My oldest son looks it over and tells me the important news in it."

"So! Your sons know how to read!"

"They can all read and write."

"So you must have sent them to school at some time?"

"No. When a boy goes to the district school for years, he not only loses his virtue but learns very little. Instead, I found a teacher who, before going to the school to teach, is willing to come by our shop early each morning. For the fee of a coffee and two para, he teaches the children for half an hour. In a year, my sons could read the Holy Qur'an and the newspaper; they also learned how to write as much as is necessary for us. In addition every year I have bought books which this teacher has recommended. During noon breaks and sometimes at night, they read these books.

"How do we live? At noon we have a break of an hour and a half. Sometimes we read the newspaper aloud, but one can do whatever one wants for that time after lunch. We shut the workshop half an hour after the call to prayer in the afternoon. In the late afternoon we take a short walk through the pleasant neighborhoods of the city. On winter nights other artisans and neighbors and their wives visit our home. The other women love my wife very much because she never gossips. Every Friday my wife, my children, and I have a picnic in our garden. So, our days pass in this way. Praise be to God that no sickness enters our home. All through our lives, only twice have I fallen ill, and my wife only three times, because we eat and sleep and get up regularly and we don't eat indiscriminately. In short, a thousand praises and thanks be to God."

CHAPTER EIGHTEEN

A Café Festivity

I was living for a while in a city in Palestine. One evening after a very hot day, I wandered through the olive groves towards an airy spot where most of the best cafés were located. The cafés were filled with people stupefied by the heat.

For some reason people like harmless lunatics. So I received a number of invitations from those sitting in the cafés to come sit and drink some coffee or smoke a water pipe with them. However, I showed no interest but, with the airs of a coquettish girl who becomes more coy the more attention is paid her, continued to walk about as I wished.

As I was passing the most elegant of the cafés, a waiter came running up to me. Nobody knows why it is that service at cafés is an art especially reserved for the Greeks, but in Syria and Palestine, though every art studio and workshop belongs to native people, the waiters in cafés and restaurants and taverns are all Greek. It was obvious from his accent that this waiter who came running towards me was also Greek.

With an odd mixture of Arabic and Turkish, he called to me, "Mirror Dede, some gentlemen are inviting you to join them; please come this way."

"Which gentlemen? Do I know them?"

He replied, "The ones sitting under those trees."

My feet were rather tired from wandering around, so in order to please these gentlemen, or rather to rest a bit and please my heart, I accepted the invitation. Even as I was known to the people of the city by my mirrors, I also was able to distinguish which of them were notables and high officials. I recognized the gentlemen in the corner as the head secretary to the district director, the superintendent of the railways, the principal of the high school, three high school teachers, and the chief engineer of the ministry of public works. When they saw me approach, they playfully stood up with great respect.

"O fellow citizen, O Mirror, Sultan! O Mirror Dede, Mirror, the Pilgrim, here please!"

Playing my part, I answered appropriately and sat down in the chair they offered me. The waiter came, and the head secretary asked, "Your majesty, the Mirror, what would you like to drink?"

I asked for a water pipe. The waiter brought it and asked again what I would like to drink.

"Bring me whatever the gentlemen are having." I said.

The waiter responded, "The gentlemen are drinking vermouth, so you would like the same?"

"Yes," I replied, "eleven big ones."

The gentlemen with me and those who spoke Turkish at nearby tables burst into laughter. When those who didn't speak Turkish inquired and found out what I had said, they too exploded with laughter.

Now the subject of conversation even at distant tables, I was being described by those who were acquainted with me as "a peculiar but harmless mad fellow."

Some foreign women were particularly impressed by my mirrors and the three rooster lollipops which I had stuck into my turban. While I was drinking my vermouth, a lovely, sexy young woman at the other side of the café who, judging by her manners was either English or American, ordered an ice cream for me. I immediately sent the waiter to her with one of the lollipops from my turban. This gesture was appreciated by everyone, and the general gaiety heightened.

Everyone applauded. Then as if the ladies were in competition with one another, they began sending me pies and cakes. I gave my other lollipops away in return, but after more offers of buns and other desserts, I stood up, gave a long cock crow, and spoke: "Ladies and gentlemen! If I had known I would come here and receive so many offerings, I would have brought a whole basket of rooster lollipops with me. Unfortunately, I brought only a few. So as a gentle reply to those who have offered things to me but could receive nothing in return and to those who may offer in the future: here, for you I'm crowing once again. This is your share."

These words of mine were immediately translated for everyone's benefit. Laughter skyrocketed. Joy and happiness overflowed; everyone was delighted in the Mirror's madness today. Just as I was about to collapse due to the foolishness and narrow vision of these heedless people, a blind woman entered the café. One could tell—by the way she walked, by the small girl at her side, by the high-quality cloth of her now worn-out dress, and by her behavior—that she had probably never begged before in her life. Perhaps not so long ago she had frequented this very café and lingered over refreshing sherberts. Returning here as a beggar must have affected her deeply. It was as if her knees could not carry her, as if she were hammered to the spot. She stood there frozen.

The miserable sight of this wretched woman, who apparently lacked the courage to step any further into the gay atmosphere, made a strong impression on me. Forgetting to play "the mad one," or rather assuming a different role, I stood up. I turned the cloth of my turban into a beggars bag and first in Turkish, then in Arabic, French, and German, called, "Ladies and gentlemen! Please give alms to this poor woman!"

Astonished, everyone threw kurush, quarters—whatever change they had—into the cloth as I went among the tables explaining the situation. In the blink of an eye, I had collected a few hundred kurush for her and put them into her hands.

After this, the gentlemen who were sitting with me dropped their mocking attitude and began to treat me with real respect. This was something I couldn't tolerate. In spite of their insistence I made up my mind to leave the café and wander about freely in my own world. However, they insisted so much I finally accepted their invitation to stay and have dinner with them, saying to myself, "Why not have a festive time like this among my souvenirs as well?"

While we were eating, the high school principal, who was sitting next to me, leaned over to speak into my ear: "My friend, one has to be really blind not to see that under this shabby masquerade there exists a well-educated, mature man with a great and generous heart. When you saw the terrible situation of that poor woman and stood up, the purity and nobility of your face made all of us obey in spite of your costume. We were charmed and impressed. In order to gather a few hundred kurush of alms in a few minutes, one has to deeply affect the spirits of those who would contribute. You accomplished this. Friend, why did you renounce the service of mankind and choose this strange way of life and this odd clothing?"

The words of this young man were so full of purity and love that I answered him: "My dear, if someone else had asked me this question, I would have dispelled it easily with a crazy answer. But because of the purity I see in your heart, I will tell you the truth. I have been betrayed so often by people that, in order not to cause them any harm, I found it preferable to pass my life pleasantly in the way in which you see me. Reflect on my words; what you make of them will be a benefit which belongs to you."

I said farewell to everyone, bowed, and returned to the quiet room of the house in which I was staying.

CHAPTER NINETEEN

The Elixir of Youth

*T*here was a noble man living among the people of a certain city in Syria. Over the years, through extravagance and generosity, he had squandered the family fortune accumulated over centuries, but still, compared to most people, he was fairly well off. Though this man had a strong build and was only sixty-five, his body was worn out from overindulgence. He had never before married but now decided to attempt it. Perhaps he thought he might still have time to taste familial happiness or wanted to raise children who might remember him after his death, though the likelihood of success at his age was rather slim.

Well, six months earlier a catastrophe had occurred, and news of it had spread throughout the area. Among the wealthy people of that time there was a strange man who himself had not had a proper upbringing. As a result, his son had become a well-known playboy, and his daughter although only thirteen had begun to make love with whomever she encountered. She had, however, finally devoted her entire existence to a certain poor but uniquely handsome boy, uniting with him alone.

Eventually, the father of the girl was informed. Although he had the right to demand that the young man marry his daughter, he decided against it for he was extremely proud and miserly; the thought of marrying his only daughter to such a poor man was not appealing. This scandal provided much food for gossip among the people of the district. One day the poor boy suddenly disappeared. A week later his body was found in a well. It was rumored that he had been killed and deliberately thrown into the well; others said that he had committed suicide because of his love and grief. The police investigated haphazardly, but as was often the case with affairs of the wealthy, everything was covered over and forgotten.

After four or five months the family decided to attempt to marry this attractive, promiscuous young woman to the older, wealthy gentleman who was looking for a wife. By marrying his daughter to such a nobleman whom no one would slander openly, the girl's father hoped to erase the memory of the young man's death and also gain access to the gentleman's substantial fortune. The father of the girl knew that a girl of fifteen could be a deadly poison for an old man.

The elderly gentleman was apparently hoping to regain some of his old glory before his life ended. Perhaps he also wanted to benefit from the fortune of his future father-in-law, whose stinginess had not yet become apparent to him.

It was rather obvious, though, that the father-in-law was the one who had the most to gain from the marriage. Every wedding gift to the young girl would be but the harbinger of others to follow after the marriage; clearly, the fortunes of the elderly gentleman would soon be depleted.

In those days, I had begun to shave carefully as though I was preparing for my final day. So I frequently dropped into the local barber shop. One day when the barber saw me, he greeted me cheerfully, "Hello! Welcome Mirror Dede!"

He invited me to sit down, and we began chatting.

The barber was a very talkative man, always interested in the affairs of his colleagues and the local people. He began, "Have you heard, Mirror Dede? Miss ___, the fiance of Mr___, wants to see him. The

133

gentleman will first come here this afternoon. Why will he come? You will say, 'It's none of my business,' won't you? Today I have a lot of work to do. I will dye his hair, beard, and moustache. I'll apply silk thread to his face to remove those extra hairs. Then I will wash his face with alum and latron water. I'll repair his wrinkles. O Mirror Dede, my alum and latron water is quite strong. Shall I spread some on your face too to repair your wrinkles? May God save you. Your face would tighten like a soldier's drum, so tight no lines would be left. A bit of latron inside gives one a mental brilliance, too. . . . So, you don't want it? Don't move your head, or you'll make me cut you.

"After I finish his make up, with his cane in hand, he will pass under the young girl's window. Look, you can keep a secret: the herbalist next door is preparing potency pills of devil's shit for the gentleman. You understand? There's no more gunpowder in the old fellow. They say that devil's shit is really strong. If I need some in my old age, I'll get some, too. I have the formula. By the way, Mirror Dede, have you ever taken pills made from devil's shit? They say it smells a bit, but anyway, what do you think about all this? This gentleman is about seventy. What does it mean to marry such a disaster of fifteen? If you ask me, when a man reaches such an age, neither devil's shit nor even goose shit would be of help. Undoubtedly he will surely die soon after he marries. The gravedigger had better dig the grave two or three meters deep, and if he doesn't die in a few weeks as we expect, if he lasts five or ten months, it will have to be dug ten times as deep."

"What's the need for such a deep grave?" I asked.

"Oh, what's the need? Will his horns be left in the air?" He burst into laughter. "If he survives a year, his horns will grow as high as the minarets of the largest mosque. If only you knew what a skillful girl she is!"

He had finished shaving me, so I said good-bye to the gossiping barber and returned home.

This elderly gentleman was actually a good man. His financial loss had adversely affected no on but him, and a large portion of his wealth had gone to comfort the poor. He was more admirable than you might have realized. He was even kind to me and with true nobility always tried to please my heart. I felt sure that he wouldn't be able to tolerate the scandals that would undoubtedly start after the marriage; I hated to see his days end so tragically, so I decided to do something for him. I thought for a while and then went shopping. I bought a small tin of gray polish and took it to my place which was at the end of the square near his house.

I loved to make excursions among the vegetable gardens along a stream at the outskirts of the city. While wandering there, I sometimes saw an old abandoned donkey. The beast, weary of life, cast amorous glances with his tired eyes. I went in search of him and finally found him near a ditch filled with water. I put the rope I had prepared around his neck and began to pull. This donkey had been diving into his own thoughts for such a long time that he had turned into a philosopher accustomed to viewing life as a transitory and empty thing. Suddenly he realized that the rope of ownership was again around his neck and, quickly becoming obstinate, attempted to reclaim his freedom. Remembering his youth, he stretched out his legs and stubbornly refused to walk, but the poor thing was really the picture of weakness. It didn't take him long to realize that resistance was of no use. Soon he became quite philosophical again and, as if to show everyone that it was necessary to surrender under such obligations, he began to follow me with slow and dignified steps. Some mischievous boys, seeing me return with the donkey, gathered into a parade behind me.

"The Mirror Dede is going to sell wood!" they screamed. By the time I had approached my place, the number of children following me had grown to more than fifty. The town fool who watched even the simplest thing with grave intensity soon joined their ranks.

Perhaps the uproar of the children attracted the nobleman's attention, for as we passed in front of his stately home, he looked out of his window. When I came to the middle of the square, I tied the donkey to a small rock and started walking towards my hut. I got some water and soap, returned to the donkey, and began washing it carefully.

The gentleman still watched me from his window. After I washed the donkey, I dried him and carefully began to rub his hair with the large piece of alum. Then I turned him towards the sun and cleaned the matted hair in his ears and on his feet. More and more spectators began to gather. They watched with great astonishment as I began to apply the gray dye. After half an hour's work, the donkey was shining like a Venetian mirror.

The gentleman's butler came over and invited me in. I had been expecting the invitation.

The gentleman greeted me joyfully and right away asked, "Mirror Dede! What are you doing? Truly, no one expects reason in your affairs, but what *is* this you are doing? Whose donkey is this? Why did you dye it?"

I replied, "Sir, this poor animal is almost twenty-four years old. That corresponds to sixty or seventy years for men. I also have a young female donkey that is five years old. I will breed them. The world has changed, and the female donkeys have changed too. Now they put on coquettish airs. The hair of that poor old donkey had fallen off; his bones were in the open, and no brightness remained in the rest of the hair he still had. I knew very well that no young female donkey would desire him. So, I dyed him with varnish that he might begin to shine like a frisky young donkey. Tomorrow, I will get some paste from the herbalist that contains devil's shit and mix it with his fodder. He will soon begin to neigh and prance like a horse! Before I dyed him, I washed him with latron and alum water. If I make him drink a little, too, his body will tighten like a drum; he'll lose his laziness and will attract the young female."

The gentleman was looking at my face in astonishment. He spoke, "Mirror Sultan, nobody takes you seriously, but this thing you have done isn't wise."

"Sir, why do you say that? A lot of old men do exactly the same thing to themselves. Donkeys have no reason. The young donkey may well be deceived by the dye and be drawn to approach her new partner. However, human beings have intelligence; their females are not so easily deceived. The men who do this sort of thing are only deceiving themselves, not the females. So, people aren't really any wiser than I am.

As for the "elixir of youth," the life of the human being is divided into phases. An elixir is a very useful thing in one's youth, but the "elixir of youth" given to an old man who has reached his maturity puts his natural life in danger. Though this is a plain truth, many aging people still experiment with elixirs. So, there really isn't anything unusual about my donkey's situation. But, for example, suppose the young donkey sees this old donkey at a distance and is deceived by his appearance and tries to unite with him; it's natural that the fraud will become apparent when they come together. What will happen after that? The young female will leave this poor old one and run away to look for a fresh young mate proper for herself, right? This poor old donkey of mine, though he is a donkey, will then pass the last of his days in jealousy and grief. Such a pity!"

As I continued speaking, the face of the gentleman began changing colors from white, to red, to white again. Wrapped in thought, he rang the bell for his servant.

"Please prepare coffee for us immediately," he said "We'll drink it with the Mirror Dede."

The coffee arrived. The gentleman had taken out a pen and some paper from a chest of drawers, and while we drank our coffee, he wrote and thought and wrote again. When he had finished, he held my hand and spoke, "Mirror Dede, your medicine was really quite bitter, but it has completely succeeded. By saving me from despair at the end of my life, you have proven that you are not a lunatic but a saint. Take this paper and read it, please."

Filled with sadness, I took the paper from him and began to read. The gentleman was informing the father of the young girl that he had decided to give up the arranged marriage for reasons of health. I stood up to go. Before saying farewell, the gentleman begged me to visit him often.

I did visit him frequently. For six months we enjoyed pleasant and useful conversations. From his words and behavior, I could see that he was really a very mature person. Not long after that he became ill. His last words were:

"My dear Mirror, I owe this world and the next world to you because you have saved me from a tragedy. If you hadn't been around, the fortune and estate that I leave behind would have become the instrument of useless pleasure for one who would have made a mockery of me; I would have writhed in torture in my grave. It is through your example and your conversation that I have realized that people have a broader family in the world than just their blood family. I am happy to see that this is the world of humanity. As I don't have any relatives, I have willed that an orphanage be founded with my remaining fortune. Now I can die comfortably."

Indeed, after his death, an orphanage was founded. On Friday nights orphans visit his grave, and the prayers[1] offered by those innocent mouths naturally make his spirit happy. May God have mercy on him.

---

1. prayers: the *Fatiha* (Surah I of the Qur'an) the quintessential prayer of the Islamic faith which is at the core of every prayer offering. It is often reflected upon at the beginning of any enterprise, as well as being recited at births and deaths and as a blessing offered at the grave of a loved one.

In the name of God, the Beneficent and Merciful.
All praise be to God, Lord of all worlds,
the infinitely Beneficent and Merciful,
Master on the day of reckoning.
You alone do we worship. You alone do we ask for help.
Guide us on the straight path,
the path of those you have blessed,
not the path of those who have brought down your wrath,
nor of those who have gone astray.

Classic Sufi literature available from Threshold:

Rumi:
Open Secret, Versions of Rumi $9
Translated by John Moyne, Coleman Barks
Unseen Rain, Quatrains $9
Translated by John Moyne, Coleman Barks
This Longing, Poetry & Letters $9
Translated by Coleman Barks, John Moyne
Feeling The Shoulder of the Lion, Poetry & Teaching Stories $9
Translated by Coleman Barks
Rumi: Daylight, A Daybook of Spiritual Guidance $19
Translated by Camille & Kabir Helminski
Love is a Stranger, Selected Lyric Poetry $9
Translated by Kabir Edmund Helminski

Other Sufi Poetry:
The Drop That Became The Sea, Yunus Emre $8
Translated by Kabir Helminski, Refik Algan
Happiness Without Death, Assad Ali $9
Translated by Helminski, Shihabi
Doorkeeper of the Heart, Versions of Rabi'a $8
Versions by Charles Upton

Other Books on Sufism:
The Most Beautiful Names $11
Shaikh Tosun Bayrak
Love is the Wine, Talks of a Sufi Master $9
Shaikh Muzaffer Ozak
What the Seeker Needs, Writings of Ibn 'Arabi $10
Translated by Bayrak & Harris
Awakened Dreams, Raji's Journeys with the Mirror Dede $13
Ahmet Hilmi, translated by Algan & C. Helminski
Inspirations on the Path of Blame $13
Shaikh Badruddin of Simawna, Translated by Bayrak

Send payment plus $3 for 1st book, $.50 each additional to:
Threshold Books, RD 4, Box 600, Putney, VT 05346
Order by phone (credit cards accepted): (802) 257-2779